The Table Talk And Opinions Of Napoleon Buonaparte... - Primary Source Edition

Napoleon I (Emperor of the French)

Nabu Public Domain Reprints:

You are holding a reproduction of an original work published before 1923 that is in the public domain in the United States of America, and possibly other countries. You may freely copy and distribute this work as no entity (individual or corporate) has a copyright on the body of the work. This book may contain prior copyright references, and library stamps (as most of these works were scanned from library copies). These have been scanned and retained as part of the historical artifact.

This book may have occasional imperfections such as missing or blurred pages, poor pictures, errant marks, etc. that were either part of the original artifact, or were introduced by the scanning process. We believe this work is culturally important, and despite the imperfections, have elected to bring it back into print as part of our continuing commitment to the preservation of printed works worldwide. We appreciate your understanding of the imperfections in the preservation process, and hope you enjoy this valuable book.

NAPOLEON BUONAPARTE.

THE TABLE TALK AND OPINIONS OF NAPOLEON BUONAPARTE.

"*Sic cogitavit.*"—Bacon.

LONDON:
SAMPSON LOW, SON, AND MARSTON.
CROWN BUILDINGS, 188, FLEET STREET.
1868.

~~5522.28.2~~
~~Fr.1570.22~~
Fr 1405.205
A

Harvard College Lib'y.
from
Miss. Longfellow,
Mrs. Dana, & Mrs. Thorp.
7 Nov. 1894

PREFACE.

THE aim of this volume is so clearly seen in its title, that few words are necessary here, and these will be used only to assure the reader, that from the mass of literature which has already grown around the history of the most extraordinary captain and statesman of modern times, the conversations, phrases and opinions which are most characteristic have been carefully gathered together, and subjected to some sort of arrangement; so that we have here, in a small compass, that which will best, without bias, form our judgment of a man who, while he has on the one hand been unduly exalted, has on the other been unjustly condemned. Judged here by his own words, by his warm opinions, his ardent wishes, his generous impulses, or his selfish and inexorable determinations, he will perhaps receive that justice which he believed posterity would accord him.

Judges of literary work will easily perceive the difficulty of adequately performing this task in so small a space. It would have been easier to have written a much larger volume, just as it is less difficult to produce several gallons of tasteless broth than one half pint of Liebig's essence of meat. It was indeed of the life of Napoleon that Sir Walter Scott declared that "he produced nine volumes because he had not time to write one." If the critics will bear this in mind, the necessity for omission of purely military and political matters and details, they will probably not complain that we have not given all the words of a great man during a busy life.

It may be as well, however, for the editor of the series, while bearing witness to the industry and judgment of the compiler, to submit a list of the chief works consulted, with a remark that were it ostentatiously paraded, it could be very largely extended.

"History of Napoleon." By J. G. Lockhart. Murray's Family Library.

"History of Napoleon." Sir Walter Scott.

"Recits de la Captivité de l'Empereur Napoleon à S^te. Hélène." Par le Comte Montholon.

"The Last Days of the Emperor Napoleon." G. Antommarchi.

Caulaincourt's "Recollections of Napoleon."

"The Entertaining History of the Early Years of Napoleon." By a Royal Emigrant.

"Private Memoirs of Napoleon." By Bourrienne.

"Memoires de Josephine."

"The Edinburgh Review." (Several volumes.)

"Memoirs of Fouché."

"The Court and Camp of Buonaparte."

"The Book of Fate of H. I. M. Napoleon."

"The Last Six Weeks of Napoleon's Life." By John Monkhouse, a Naval Officer.

"History of a Visit to St. Helena." By Mrs. Ward. (Privately printed.)

Various pamphlets, reviews, private memoirs, &c.

TABLE TALK AND OPINIONS OF NAPOLEON THE FIRST.

1773.

WHEN Napoleon was about fourteen, he was conversing with a lady about Marshal Turenne, and extolling him to the skies.

"Yes, my friend," she answered, "he was a great man; but I should like him better if he had not burnt the Palatinate."

"What does that matter," he replied briskly, "if the burning was necessary to the success of his plans?"

Napoleon's German master, a heavy and phlegmatic man, who thought the study of German the only necessary to a man's success in life, finding Napoleon absent from his class one day, asked where he was. He was told he was undergoing his examination for the artillery.

"Does he know anything then?" he asked ironically.

"Why, sir, he is the best mathematician in the school."

"Well," was his sage remark, "I have always heard say, and I always thought, that mathematics was a study only suitable to fools."

"It would be satisfactory to know," Napoleon said twenty years after, "if my professor of languages lived long enough to enjoy his discernment."

In 1782, at one of the holiday school *fêtes* at Brienne, to which all the inhabitants of the place were invited, guards were established to preserve order. The dignities of officer and subaltern were conferred only on the most distinguished. Bonaparte was one of these on a certain occasion, when "The Death of Cæsar" was to be performed. A janitor's wife who was perfectly well known presented herself for admission without a ticket. She made a clamour, and insisted upon being let in, and the sergeant reported her to Napoleon, who, in an imperative tone, exclaimed, "Let that woman be removed, who brings into this place the licence of a camp."

Bonaparte was confirmed at the military school at Paris. At the name of Napoleon, the archbishop who confirmed him, expressed his astonishment, saying that he did not know this saint, that he was not in the calendar, &c. The child answered unhesitatingly, "That that was no reason, for there were a crowd of saints in Paradise, and only 365 days in the year."[1]

Dining one day with one of the professors at Brienne, the professor knowing his young pupil's admiration for Paoli, spoke disrespectfully of the general to tease the boy. Napoleon was energetic in his defence. "Paoli,

---

[1] In a little volume, published about 1802, entitled "Authentic Memoirs of Bonaparte, First Consul of the French Republic, from his birth to the present time," the anecdote is finished as follows:—"Napoleon," the assistant minister remarked to the prelate, "I do not know that saint." "I believe it," replied Napoleon; "the *saint* is a CORSICAN!"

sir," said he, " was a great man! he loved his country; and I shall never forgive my father for consenting to the union of Corsica with France."

Speaking of his early attachment to Mademoiselle du Colombier, Napoleon said, "We were the most innocent creatures imaginable. We contrived short interviews together. I well remember one which took place on a midsummer's morning, just as the light began to dawn. It will hardly be believed that all our happiness consisted in eating cherries together."

1790. When at Auxonne, Napoleon and some subaltern officers were quartered at the house of a barber. Napoleon, as usual when off duty, shut himself in his room and devoted himself to study. The other young officers amused themselves by coquetting with the barber's pretty wife, who was much annoyed that her charms had no power to draw Napoleon from his studies. Afterwards, when in command of the army in Italy, Napoleon passed through Auxonne, on his way to Marengo. He stopped at the barber's door, and asked his former hostess if she remembered a young officer by the name of Bonaparte, who once quartered in her family.

"Indeed I do," she replied pettishly; "and a very disagreeable young man he was. He was always shut up in his room, and if he did walk out, he never condescended to speak to any one."

"Ah! my good woman!" Napoleon rejoined, "had I passed my time as you wished to have me, I should not now have been in command of the army of Italy."

One evening, just after the demolition of the Bastile, Napoleon, in M. Neckar's drawing-room, in a long speech which he made, much to the astonishment of every one, said, "If our troops are not compelled unhesitatingly to obey the commands of the executive, we shall be exposed to the blind fury of democratic passions, which will render France the most miserable country on the globe. The ministry may be assured that if the daily increasing arrogance of the Parisian mob is not repressed by a strong arm, and social order rigidly maintained, we shall see not only this capital, but every other city in France, thrown into a state of indescribable anarchy, while the real friends of liberty, the enlightened patriots now working for the best good of our country, will sink beneath a set of demagogues, who, with louder outcries for freedom on their tongues, will be in reality but a horde of savages worse than the Neros of old."

1792. While in Paris, on the 20th of June, Napoleon was walking with Bourrienne on the banks of the Seine. They followed the multitude, and saw them swarm into the Tuileries, drag the humiliated king into the embrasure of a window, and force him to put the red cap on his head. Napoleon turned from the sight, exclaiming, "The wretches! how could they suffer this vile mob to enter the palace! They should have swept down the first five hundred with grape shot, and the rest would have soon taken to flight."

"I frankly declare," said Napoleon, "that if I were compelled to choose between the old monarchy and Jacobin misrule, I should infinitely prefer the former."

One evening, in the midst of the Reign of Terror, on returning from a walk through the streets of Paris, a lady asked him—

"How do you like the new Constitution?"

He replied hesitatingly,

"Why, it is good in one sense certainly; but all that is connected with carnage is bad;" and then he exclaimed in an outburst of undisguised feeling, "No! no! no! down with this constitution; I do not like it!"

1794. During the siege of Toulon, one of the agents of the Convention ventured to criticise the position of a gun which Napoleon was superintending. "Do you," he tartly replied, "attend to your duty as national commissioners, and I will be answerable for mine with my head."

Napoleon's younger brother Louis visited him during this siege. They went together one morning to a place where a fruitless assault had been made, and two hundred Frenchmen were dead upon the ground. On beholding them, Napoleon exclaimed, "All those men have been needlessly sacrificed. Had intelligence commanded here, none of these lives need have been lost. Learn from this, my brother, how indispensable and imperatively necessary it is that those should possess knowledge who aspire to assume the command over others."

"General," said Bonaparte to Dugommier, as he raised the tri-coloured flag over the crumbling walls of the rampart, "go and sleep. We have taken Toulon."

An officer, entering Napoleon's room, found, much to his astonishment, Napoleon dressed and studying.

"What!" exclaimed his friend, "are you not in bed yet?"

"In bed!" replied Napoleon. "I have finished my sleep, and already risen."

"What, so early!" the other replied.

"Yes," continued Napoleon, "so early. Two or three hours of sleep are enough for any man."

Napoleon had a great contempt for the effeminate young men of his time. He exclaimed one day, "Can it be that upon such creatures Fortune is willing to lavish her favours! How contemptible is human nature!"

When Barras introduced Napoleon to the Convention as a fit man to be entrusted with the command, the President asked,

"Are you willing to undertake the defence of the Convention?"

"Yes," was the reply.

After a time the President continued—

"Are you aware of the magnitude of the undertaking?"

"Perfectly," replied Napoleon, fixing his eyes upon his questioner; "and I am in the habit of accomplishing that which I undertake."

"How could you," a lady asked him about this time, "fire thus mercilessly upon your countrymen?"

"A soldier," he replied calmly, "is only a machine to obey orders. This is *my seal* which I have impressed upon Paris."

Napoleon's apt replies often excited good humour in a crowd.

A large and brawny fishwoman once was haranguing the mob, and telling them not to disperse. She finished by exclaiming, "Never mind those coxcombs with epaulets on their shoulders; they care not if we poor people all starve, if they can but feed well and grow fat."

Napoleon, who was as thin as a shadow, turned to her and said, "Look at me, my good woman, and tell me which of us two is the fatter."

The fishfag was completely disconcerted, and the crowd dispersed.

1796. "Good God!" Napoleon said in Italy, whilst residing at Montebello, "how rare men are. There are eighteen millions in Italy, and I have with difficulty found two, Dandolo and Melzi."

"Europe!" Napoleon exclaimed at Passeriano, "Europe is but a molehill; there never have existed mighty empires, there never have occurred great revolutions, save in the East, where live six hundred millions of men —the cradle of all religions, the birth-place of all metaphysics."

The night following the battle of Arcola, Bonaparte disguised himself in the dress of an inferior officer, and traversed the camp. He found a sentinel leaning on the butt end of his musket, fast asleep. He gently placed his head on the ground, and kept watch for him for two hours. When the soldier woke and discovered Napoleon himself doing duty for him, he was terror-stricken. "The General! Bonaparte!" he exclaimed; "I am then undone."

Bonaparte, with the greatest gentleness, replied, "Not so, fellow-soldier; recover yourself; after so much fatigue, a brave man like you may be allowed to sleep awhile; but in future choose your time better."

Just before his marriage Napoleon received the appointment of Commander-in-chief of the army of Italy; he was then twenty-six. "You are rather young," said one of the directors, "to assume responsibilities so weighty, and to take the command over veteran generals."

"In one year," Napoleon replied, "I shall be old or dead."

"We can place you in command of men only," said Carnot, "for the troops require everything, and we can furnish you with no money to provide supplies."

"Give me only men enough," Napoleon answered, "and I ask for nothing more; I will be answerable for the result."

"My extreme youth when I took command of the army of Italy," Napoleon remarked afterwards, "made it necessary for me to evince great reserve of manners, and the utmost severity of morals. This was indispensable to enable me to sustain authority over men so greatly superior in age and experience. I pursued a line of conduct in the highest degree irreproachable and exemplary. In spotless morality I was a Cato, and must have appeared such to all. I was a philosopher and a sage. My supremacy could be retained only by proving myself a better man than any other man in the army. Had I yielded to human weaknesses I should have lost my power."

At the first interview between Napoleon and the veteran generals whom he was to command, Rampon undertook to give the young commander some advice. Napoleon, who was impatient of advice, exclaimed, "Gentlemen, the art of war is in its infancy. The time has passed in which enemies are mutually to appoint the place of combat, advance hat in hand, and say, ' *Gentlemen, will you have the goodness to fire!*' We must cut the enemy in pieces, precipitate ourselves, like a torrent, upon their battalions, and grind them to powder. Experienced generals conduct the troops opposed to us! So much the better! so much the better! Their experience will not avail them against me. Mark my words, they will soon burn their books on tactics, and know not what to do. Yes, gentlemen! the first onset of the Italian army will give birth to a new epoch in military affairs. As for us, we must hurl ourselves on the foe like a thunderbolt, and smite like it. Disconcerted by our tactics, and not daring to put them into execution, they will fly before us as the shades of night before the uprising sun."

" My title of nobility dates from the battle of Montenotte," said Napoleon to the Emperor of Austria.

Napoleon sent the celebrated picture of St. Jerome from the Duke of Parma's gallery to the Museum at Paris. The duke, to save his work of art, offered Napoleon two hundred thousand dollars, which the conqueror refused to take, saying: "The sum which he offers us will soon be spent; but the possession of such a masterpiece at Paris will adorn that capital for ages, and give birth to similar exertions of genius."

"It is impossible," said an officer at Lodi, "that any men can force their way across that narrow bridge, in the face of such an annihilating storm of balls as must be encountered."

"How! impossible!" exclaimed Napoleon; "that word is not French."

"Neither the quelling of the sections," said Napoleon, "nor the victory of Montenotte, induced me to think myself a superior character. It was not till after the *terrible passage of the bridge of Lodi* that the idea entered my mind that I might become a decisive actor in the political arena. Then arose for the first time the spark of great ambition."

"Different matters are arranged in my head," said Napoleon, "as in drawers; I open one drawer and close another as I wish. I have never been kept awake by an involuntary pre-occupation of the mind. If I desire repose, I shut up all the drawers, and sleep. I have always slept when I wanted rest, and almost at will."

While at Milan, Napoleon had just mounted his horse one morning, when a dragoon, bearing important despatches, presented himself before him.

"Napoleon gave a verbal answer, and ordered the courier to take it back in all speed.

"I have no horse," the man answered; "I rode mine so hard that it fell dead at your palace gates."

Napoleon alighted. "Take mine," he said.

The man hesitated.

"You think him too magnificently caparisoned and too fine an animal," said Napoleon. "Nothing is too good for a French soldier."

"Pavia," said Napoleon, "is the only place I ever gave up to pillage. I promised that the soldiers should have it at their mercy for twenty-four hours; but after three hours, I could bear such scenes of outrage no longer, and put an end to them. Policy and morality are equally opposed to the system. Nothing is so certain to disorganise and completely ruin an army."

"I have," said Napoleon, "a taste for founding, not for possessing. My riches consist in glory and celebrity. The Simplon and the Louvre were, in the eyes of the people and of foreigners, more my property than any private domains could possibly have been."

1797. The Directory sent General Clarke as an envoy to Napoleon's head-quarters, to conduct negotiations with the Austrians. "If you come here to obey me," said Bonaparte, "I shall always see you with pleasure; if not, the sooner you return to those who sent you the better."

To General Clarke, on the death of his nephew, at Arcola, Napoleon wrote:—

"Your nephew Elliot has been slain upon the battlefield. That young man has several times marched at the head of our columns. He has died gloriously, and in face of the enemy; he did not have a moment's suffering. Where is the *reasonable man* who would not envy such a death? Where is he who, in the vicissitudes of life, would not give himself up to leave in this manner a world so often ungrateful?" &c.

Napoleon had no tendencies to gallantry. Madame de Staël once said to him, "It is reported that you are not very partial to the ladies."

"I am very fond of my wife, Madame," was his laconic reply.

"The English," said Napoleon, "appear to prefer the bottle to the society of their ladies; as is exemplified by dismissing the ladies from the table, and remaining for hours to drink and intoxicate themselves. If I were in England, I should decidedly leave the table with the ladies. If the object is to talk instead of to drink, why banish them? Surely conversation is never so lively nor so witty as when ladies take a part in it. Were I an Englishwoman I should feel very discontented at being turned out by the men to wait for two or three hours while they were drinking. In France, society is nothing unless ladies are present. They are the life of conversation."

The Austrian Peace Commissioners had set down as the first article in their treaty that the emperor recognized the French Republic.

"Strike that out!" said Napoleon. "The Republic is like the sun; none but the blind can fail to see it. We are our own masters, and shall establish any government we prefer." "If the French people should one day wish to create a monarchy," he afterwards remarked, "the emperor might object that he had recognized a Republic."

One of the Austrian commissioners concluded an insulting apostrophe by saying, "Austria wishes for peace, and she will severely condemn the negotiator who sacrifices the interest and repose of his country to military ambition."

Napoleon listened calmly, then rising and taking a beautiful vase in his hand, he replied, "Gentlemen, the truce is broken; war is declared; but remember, in three months I will demolish your monarchy, as I now shatter this porcelain," and he dashed the vase to fragments."

"I conquer provinces," said Napoleon; "but Josephine wins hearts."

"Truly," said Napoleon, at Milan, "I have something else to think of than love. No man wins triumphs in that way without forfeiting some palms of glory. I have traced out my plan, and the finest eyes in the world—and there are some very fine ones here—shall not make me deviate a hair's breadth from it."

A lady of rank once said to him, "What is life worth if one cannot be General Bonaparte?"
Napoleon answered her wisely: "Madame! one may be a dutiful wife, and the good mother of a family."

Travelling through Switzerland, Napoleon was greeted with such enthusiasm that Bourrienne said to him, "It must be delightful to be greeted with such demonstrations of enthusiastic admiration."
"Bah!" replied Napoleon; "this same unthinking crowd, under a slight change of circumstances, would follow me just as eagerly to the scaffold."

Bidding adieu to his troops, Napoleon said, "Soldiers! I leave you to-morrow. In separating myself from the army, I am consoled with the thought that I shall soon meet you again, and engage with you in new enterprizes. Soldiers! when conversing among yourselves of the kings you have vanquished, of the people upon whom you have conferred liberty, of the victories you have won in two campaigns, say, 'In the next two we will accomplish still more.'"

At the magnificent court of the Luxembourg, on the delivery of the treaty of Campo Formio, on the 10th of December, 1797, Napoleon replied to Talleyrand's speech thus: "Citizens! the French people, in order to be free, had kings to combat. To obtain a constitution founded on reason, it had the prejudices of eighteen centuries to overcome. Priestcraft, feudalism, despotism, have for two thousand years successively governed Europe. From the peace you have just concluded dates the era of representative governments. You have succeeded in organizing the great nation, whose vast territory is circumscribed only, because Nature herself has fixed its limits. You have done more. The two finest countries in Europe, formerly so renowned for the arts, the sciences, and the illustrious men whose cradle they were, see, with the greatest hopes, genius and freedom issuing from the tomb of their ancestors. I have the honour to deliver to you the treaty signed at Campo Formio, and ratified by the emperor. Peace secures the liberty, the prosperity, and the glory of the Republic. As soon as the happiness of France is secured by the best organic laws, the whole of Europe will be free."

Speaking of the Theophilanthropists, Napoleon said, "They can accomplish nothing; they are merely actors."

"What!" was the reply; "do you thus stigmatise those whose tenets inculcate universal benevolence and the moral virtues?"

"All moral systems are fine," rejoined Napoleon. "The Gospel alone has shown a full and complete assemblage of the principles of morality, stripped of all absurdity. It is not made up, like your creed, of a few commonplace sentences put into bad verse. Do you wish to find out the really sublime? Repeat the Lord's Prayer.

Such enthusiasts are only to be met with the weapons of ridicule; all their efforts will prove ineffectual."

Returning to Paris after a survey of the English coast, Bourrienne asked him if he considered the enterprize against England feasible.

"No; it is too hazardous," Napoleon replied. "I will not undertake it. I will not risk on such a stake the fate of our beautiful France."

The revolutionary government was in the habit of celebrating with great rejoicing the anniversary of the king's death,—the 21st of January. Napoleon was urged to honour the festival with his presence. He emphatically declined. "This *fête*," said he, " commemorates a melancholy event—a tragedy, and can only be agreeable to a few. It is right to celebrate victories; but victims left upon the field of battle are to be lamented. To celebrate the anniversary of a man's death is an act unworthy of a government; it irritates instead of calming; it shakes a government to its foundations instead of strengthening it."

1798. "I worked all day," said a man to Napoleon, as an apology for not having completed his assigned duty.

"But had you not the night also?" Napoleon suggested.

Napoleon said to Bourrienne, on the 29th of January, "Bourrienne, I shall remain here no longer; they do not want me; there is no good to be done; they will not listen to me. I see, if I loiter here I am done for quickly. Here everything grows flat; my glory is already on the wane. This little Europe of yours cannot supply the demand. We must to the East; all great reputations come from that quarter. But I will first take a turn round the coast to assure myself what can be done. I will take you with me,—you, Lannes, and Sulkowsky. If the success of a descent upon England appear doubtful, as I fear, the army of England shall become the army of the East, and I am off for Egypt."

"Now, sir," said he to another, "use dispatch. Remember that the world only took six days to create. Ask me for whatever you please, except *time*; that is the only thing which is beyond my power."

"Before the departure for Egypt, Napoleon made the following proclamation to his troops:—
"Soldiers! you have made war in mountains, plains, and cities. It remains to make it on the ocean. The Roman legions, whom you have often imitated but not yet equalled, combated Carthage by turns on the seas and on the plains of Zama. Victory never deserted their standards, because they never ceased to be brave, patient, and united. Soldiers! the eyes of Europe are upon you. You have great destinies to accomplish, battles to fight, dangers and fatigues to overcome. You are about to do more than you yet have done for the prosperity of your country, the happiness of man, and for your own glory."

Napoleon expressed his contempt for the directors in strong terms. "They cannot long retain their position," he said. "They know not how to do anything for the imagination of the nation."

Bourrienne asked Napoleon, before the expedition started, if he had really determined to risk his fate in Egypt. "Yes," was his reply; "if I stay here, I shall have to upset this miserable government, and make myself king. But we must not think of that yet. The pear is not yet ripe. I have sounded, but the time is not yet come. I must first dazzle these gentlemen by my exploits."

"My young friends," said Napoleon once to the pupils of a school he was visiting, "every hour of time is a chance of misfortune for future life."

Just before disembarking, Napoleon had the following proclamation issued to his troops: "Soldiers! you are about to undertake a conquest fraught with incalculable effects upon the commerce and civilization of the world. You will inflict upon England the most grievous stroke she can sustain before receiving her death-blow. The people with whom we are about to live are Mohammedans. Their first article of faith is, 'There is but one God, and Mohammed is his prophet.' Contradict them not. Treat them as you have the Italians and the Jews. Show the same regard to their Muftis and Imams as you have shown to the Bishops and Rabbis. Manifest for the ceremonies of the Koran the same respect you have shown to the convents and synagogues,—to the religion of Moses and that of Jesus Christ. All religions were protected by the legions of Rome. You will here find customs greatly at variance with those of Europe. Accustom yourselves to respect them. Women are not treated here as with us; but in every country he who violates is a monster. Plunder only enriches a few, while it dishonours an army, destroys its resources, and makes enemies of those whom it is the interest of all to attach as friends."

Writing to Kleber, the general-in-chief said, "The Christians will always be our friends; we must take care they do not become too insolent, lest the Turks conceive against *us* the same fanaticism as against the *Christians*. This would render them irreconcileable to *us*." Again, writing at a later period to Menon, he adds, "I thank you for the honours you have paid to *our Prophet*."*

"I never," said Napoleon, after his return from Egypt, "followed any of the tenets of the Mohammedan religion. I never prayed in the mosques. I never abstained from wine, or was circumcised. I said merely, that we were friends of the Mussulman, and that I respected their Prophet, which was true; I respect him now."

"It is not written on high that I am to perish by the hands of the Arabs," said Napoleon, after an escape from a troop of Arab horsemen.

Approaching Cairo, the glittering sun-gilded minarets of the city upon their left, and the gigantic pyramids upon their right, the army halted, and Napoleon, pointing to those lofty antiquities, exclaimed, "Soldiers! from those summits forty centuries contemplate your actions."

---

* Referring to this and Napoleon's frequent conversations with the Mohammedan priesthood, Bourrienne says, "If Bonaparte ever spoke as a Mussulman, he did so in the capacity of a military and political chief in a Mahometan country... In India he would have been for Ali, for the Dalai Lama in Thibet, or Confucius in China."

"I never passed the desert," said Napoleon, some time after, "without experiencing very painful emotions. It was the image of immensity to my thoughts. It showed no limits. It had neither beginning nor end. It was an ocean for the foot of man."

"Never yet, I believe," said Napoleon, "has there been such devotion shown by soldiers to their general as mine have displayed towards me. At Arcola, Colonel Muiron threw himself before me, covered my body with his own, and received the blow which was intended for me. He fell at my feet, and his blood spouted up in my face. In all my misfortunes never has the soldier been wanting in fidelity—never has man been served more faithfully by his troops. With the last drop of blood gushing from their veins, they cried 'Vive Napoleon!'"

"Victory," said Napoleon, "belongs to the most persevering."

Of Prince Charles, with whom he fought repeated and desperate battles in his march upon Vienna, Napoleon said, "He is a *good man*, which includes everything when said of a prince. He is incapable of a dishonourable action."

1798. On receiving intelligence from Desaix in Upper Egypt, of the loss of a very fine dgerm, called "The Italy," Napoleon said to Bourrienne, "My good friend, Italy is lost to France—it is all over—my presentiments never deceive me." "The prediction was soon realized," remarks Bourrienne.

"Bonaparte announced his entrance into Cairo," says Bourrienne, "by one of those lying bulletins that imposed only on fools. 'I bring,' said he, in this precious document, 'many prisoners and colours. I have razed the palace of the Djezzar, the ramparts of Acre. There stands not one stone upon another. All the inhabitants fled by sea; Djezzar is dangerously wounded.' I avow a painful sensation felt while writing these words from his dictation." Bourrienne continues, "It was difficult to refrain hazarding some observation; but his constant reply was, 'My dear fellow, you are a ninny, and comprehend nothing at all of the matter,' and with these words he signed what was to fill the world and inspire the historian!"

1799. "What a solace must Christianity be," said Napoleon, "to one who has an undoubting conviction of its truth." At another time he exclaimed, "The religion of Jesus is a threat, that of Mohammed a promise."

"I frankly confess," said Napoleon again and again, "that if I must choose between Bourbon oppression and mob violence, I infinitely prefer the former."

"Friendship," said Napoleon, according to Bourrienne, "is but a name. I love no one; no, not even my brothers. Joseph, perhaps, a little. And if I do love him, it is because he is my elder, and from habit. Duroc! ah yes, I love him too. But why? His character pleases me. He is cold, reserved, and resolute, and I really believe that he never shed a tear. As to myself, I know well that I have not one true friend. As long as I continue what I am, I may have as many pretended friends as I please. We must leave sensibility to the women; it is their business. Men should be firm in heart and in purpose, or they should have nothing to do with war or government. I am not amiable; no, I am not amiable. I never have been, but I am just."

On board ship, in the midst of a party of atheistical officers, Napoleon suddenly stopped before them, and said, in tones of great dignity, "Gentlemen, your arguments are very fine, but who made all those worlds, beaming so gloriously above us? Can you tell me that?"

"Rousseau was a bad man," said Napoleon, "a very bad man; he caused the revolution." When invited to Rousseau's hermitage to see his cap, table, arm chair, &c., he exclaimed, "Bah! I have no taste for such fooleries. Show them to my brother Louis. He is worthy of them."

"It is always the greater number which defeats the less," said Napoleon.

"And yet," said Gohier, "with small armies you have frequently defeated large ones."

"Even then," replied Napoleon, "it was always the inferior force which was defeated by the superior. When with a small body of men I was in the presence of a large one, collecting my little band, I fell like lightning on one of the wings of the hostile army, and defeated it. Profiting by the disorder which such an event never failed to occasion in their whole line, I repeated the attack, with similar success, in another quarter, still with my whole force. I thus beat it in detail. The general victory which was the result, was still an example of the truth of the principle, that the greater force defeats the lesser."

"I want more head and less tongue," said Napoleon, when filling the varied departments of state.

It was proposed to make Napoleon Grand Elector, with a revenue of one million dollars. "Can you conceive," he exclaimed, "that a man of the least talent or honour would humble himself to accept an office, the duties of which are merely to fatten like a pig on so many millions a year?"

1800. "I did not usurp the crown," said Napoleon proudly. "It was lying in the mire. I picked it up. The people placed it on my head."

When Murat proposed for the hand of Napoleon's sister Caroline, "Murat! Murat!" said Napoleon, "he is the son of an innkeeper. In the elevated rank to which I have attained, I cannot mix my blood with his." For a moment he appeared lost in thought, and then continued, "Besides, there is no hurry. I shall see by and by."

After the battle of Marengo, when Napoleon heard of the death of Desaix, he said, "France has lost one of her most able defenders, and I my best friend. No one has ever known how much goodness there was in Desaix's heart, and how much genius in his head." Then after a short silence, with the tears starting into his eyes, he added, "My brave Desaix always wished to die thus; but death should not have been so ready to execute his wish."

As Napoleon beheld the melancholy procession of the wounded, after the battle of Marengo, he exclaimed, "We can but regret not being wounded like these unhappy men, that we might share their sufferings."

1801. When a treaty of peace was concluded with England, Cambacères said, "Now we must make a treaty of commerce, and remove all subjects of dispute between the two countries."

Napoleon replied, "Not so fast! The political peace is made; so much the better. Let us enjoy it. As to a commercial peace, we will make one if we can. *But at no price will I sacrifice French industry.* I remember the misery of 1786."

"The old privileged classes and the foreign cabinets," said Napoleon, "hate me worse than they did Robespierre."

"My religion is very simple," Napoleon said to Monge one day. "I look at this universe, so vast, so complex, so magnificent, and I say to myself that it cannot be the result of chance, but the work, however intended, of an unknown omnipotent being, as superior to man as the universe is superior to the finest machines of human invention. Search the philosophers, and you will not find a stronger or more decisive argument. But this truth is too succinct for man. He wishes to know respecting himself and respecting his future destiny, a crowd of secrets which the universe does not disclose. Allow religion to inform him of that which he feels the need of knowing, and respect her disclosures."

Once Napoleon remarked, "What render me most hostile to the establishment of the Catholic worship, are the numerous festivals formally observed. A saint's day is a day of idleness, and I do not wish for that. People must labour in order to live. I shall consent to four holidays during the year, but no more. If the gentlemen from Rome are not satisfied with that, they may take their departure."

"The French people must be allured back to religion, not shocked," Napoleon replied to the Pope's legate, who was strenuously urging some of the most arrogant assumptions of the Papal Church. "To declare the Catholic religion the religion of the state is impossible. It is contrary to the ideas prevalent in France, and will never be admitted. In place of this declaration we can only substitute the avowal of the fact *that the Catholic religion is the religion of the majority of Frenchmen.* But there must be perfect freedom of opinion. The amalgamation of wise and honest men of all parties is the principle of my government. I must apply that principle to the Church as well as to the State. It is the only way of putting an end to the troubles of France, and I shall persist in it undeviatingly."

1802. "France needs nothing so much to promote her regeneration," said the First Consul, " as good mothers."

"Rewards are not to be conferred upon soldiers alone," said Napoleon; " all sorts of merits are brothers. The courage of the president of the Convention resisting the populace should be compared with the courage of Kleber mounting to the assault of Acre. It is right that civil as well as military virtues should have their reward; intelligence has rights before force. Force, without intelligence, is nothing."

In answer to the deputation that met to pass a eulogium upon Napoleon's splendid achievements, he replied as follows:—

"I receive with sincere gratitude the wish expressed by the Tribunate. I desire no other glory than that of having completely performed the task imposed upon me. I seek no reward but the affection of my fellow citizens. I shall be satisfied if they are convinced that my greatest misfortunes will always be the evils they may experience; that life is only dear to me as long as I can render services to my country; and that death will have no bitterness for me, if my last looks can see the happiness of the Republic as firmly secured as its glory."

1804. A young English sailor who had escaped from a prison in the interior of France, had succeeded in reaching the coast near Boulogne. Here he made a little skiff, miserably frail, of the branches and bark of trees. This bark he intended to cross the Channel in.

"Did you really intend," Napoleon said, "to brave the terrors of the ocean in so frail a skiff?"

"Yes," said the young man, "with your permission I will embark immediately."

"Have you a sweetheart at home," asked Napoleon, "that you are so desirous to go to your country again?"

"No," replied the lad, "but I wish to see my mother, who is aged, poor, and infirm."

Napoleon's heart was touched. "You shall see her," he answered, "and give her this purse of gold from me. She can be no common woman to have brought up so good a son."

When Napoleon pardoned Polignac, at his wife's earnest entreaties, he said to her:

"I am surprised at finding Armand Polignac, my old school-companion, plotting against my life. I will, however, grant his pardon to the tears of his wife. I only hope that this act of weakness on my part may not encourage fresh acts of imprudence. Those princes, madame, are most deeply culpable who thus compromise the lives of their faithful servants, without partaking their perils."

Bourrienne, conversing with Napoleon one day, remarked that he thought it impossible for him to become recognized among the old reigning families of Europe.

"If it comes to that," Napoleon answered, "I will dethrone them all, and then I shall be the oldest reigning sovereign."

When Napoleon accepted the title of emperor, he briefly replied in the following terms:—

"Everything which can contribute to the weal of the country is essentially connected with my happiness. I accept the title which you believe to be useful to the glory of the nation. I submit to the people the sanction of the law of hereditary succession. I hope that France will never repent the honours with which she shall invest my family. At all events, my spirit will no longer be with my posterity on that day when it shall cease to merit the love and confidence of the Grand Nation."

"Off! off with these confounded trappings," Napoleon exclaimed after his coronation, throwing mantle and robe into various corners of the room. "I never passed such tedious hours before."

1805. As the Emperor and Empress were crossing, Napoleon alighted and proceeded some distance on foot, when he met a peasant woman.

"Where are you going in such haste this morning?" he asked.

"To see the Emperor," she replied. "They tell me the Emperor is to pass this way."

"And why do you wish to see him," said Napoleon, "what have you done but exchange one tyrant for another? You have had the Bourbons, now you have Napoleon."

"No matter," answered the woman; "Napoleon is our king; but the Bourbons were the kings of the *nobles*."

"This," said Napoleon, when he related the anecdote; "this comprehends the whole matter."

On one occasion a soldier of the consular guard committed suicide from a disappointment in love. Napoleon issued the following order of the day:—

"The grenadier Gobain has committed suicide from love. He was in other respects an excellent soldier. This is the second incident of the kind within a month. The First Consul directs it to be inserted in the order-book of the guard, that a soldier ought to know how to vanquish the pangs and melancholy of the passions; that there is as much true courage in bearing up against mental sufferings with constancy, as in remaining firm on the wall of a battery. To yield ourselves to grief without resistance, or to kill ourselves to escape affliction, is to abandon the field of battle before the victory is gained."

After the battle of Austerlitz, the Emperor Francis of Austria visited Napoleon to make negotiations for himself and Alexander of Russia. When he had succeeded and gone, Napoleon walked hurriedly to and fro for a time, and after a short silence he was heard to say, "I have acted very unwisely. I could have followed up my victory, and taken the whole of the Austrian and Russian armies. They are both entirely in my power. But—let it be. It will at least cause some less tears to be shed."

When Napoleon declared his intention to send Frederic the Great's sword to the Invalides, to please the old soldiers, General Rapp suggested that he should keep it for himself. Napoleon looked at the general, with a half-reproachful, half-comical expression, and replied, "Have I not a sword of my own, Mr. Giver-of-Advice?"

While at Eylau an orderly officer, sent with despatches to the Emperor, was a long time on the road. Napoleon sent for him.

"Sir," said he severely, as the officer entered, "at what hour were these despatches placed in your hands?"

"At eight o'clock in the evening, sire."

"And how many leagues had you to ride?"

"I do not know precisely, sire."

"But you ought to know. An orderly officer ought to know that. I know. You had twenty-seven miles to ride, and you set off at eight o'clock. Look at your watch, sir. What o'clock is it now?"

"Half-past twelve, sire. The roads were in a terrible state. In some places the snow blocked up the path—"

"Poor excuses, sir, poor excuses. Retire, and await my orders." As the officer closed the door he exclaimed,—

"This cool, leisurely gentlemen, wants stimulating."

When the answer was ready, the officer was recalled.

"Set off immediately, sir," said Napoleon, "these despatches must be delivered with the utmost speed. General Lasalle must receive my orders by three o'clock—by three o'clock, you understand, sir?"

"Sire," was the reply, "by half-past two the general shall have the orders of which I have the honour to be the bearer."

As he was leaving the room, Napoleon called him back, and said in his kindest and most winning voice, "Tell General Lasalle that it will be agreeable to me that you should be the person selected to announce to me the success of these movements."

"To a father," said Napoleon, "who loses his children, victory has no charms. When the heart speaks, glory itself is an illusion."

1807. While at Osterode, Napoleon wrote to the Minister of the Interior :—

"An effective mode of encouraging literature would be to establish a journal with an enlightened criticism, free from that coarse brutality which characterizes the existing newspapers, and which is so contrary to the true interests of the nation. Journals now never criticise with the intention of repressing mediocrity, guiding inexperience, or encouraging rising merit. All their endeavour is to wither, to destroy. Articles should be selected for the journals where reasoning is mingled with eloquence, where praise for deserved merit is tempered with censure for faults. Merit, however inconsiderable, should be sought for and rewarded."

During the battle at Friedland, a young soldier instinctively dodged as a cannon ball came whistling over his head. Napoleon smiled, and said to him, "My friend, if that ball were destined for you it would be sure to find you, though you were to burrow a hundred feet under ground."

"My soldiers," said Napoleon to the Czar, "are as brave as it is possible to be, but they are too much addicted to reasoning on their position. If they had the impassible firmness and docility of the Russians, the world would be too small for their exploits."

"Gentlemen," said Napoleon, addressing the council upon one occasion. "War is not a profession of ease and comfort. Quietly seated on your benches here, you know it only by reading our bulletins, or hearing of our triumphs. You know nothing of our nightly watches, our forced marches, the sufferings and privations of every kind to which we are exposed. But I do know them, for I witness, and sometimes share them."

On Napoleon's thirty-eighth birthday, a brilliant party was assembled at the Tuileries. Taking the arm of his faithful friend, Duroc, he wandered about the gardens in disguise. A little boy was shouting, Vive l'Empereur! Napoleon took the child in his arms and asked him why he shouted so.

"Because my father and mother taught me to love and bless the Emperor," the child answered.

Napoleon then spoke to the parents, who testified to the blessings Napoleon had conferred upon France. The next day a present from the Emperor informed them to whom they had unbosomed their gratitude.

One day, when on a visit to the female school he had founded at Ecouen, he playfully asked a bright young girl, "How many needlefuls of thread does it take to make a shirt?"

She replied wittily, "One, sire, if it were sufficiently long."

Napoleon was so pleased with the reply, that he gave the young lady a gold chain.

"A woman turns the head of the Autocrat of all the Russias," Napoleon said, referring to the Emperor Alexander. "All the women in the world would not make me lose an hour. Continue to acquaint me of everything. Let me know the smallest details. The private life of a man is a mirror in which we may see many useful lessons reflected."

1808. Speaking of the German drama, in which tragedy and comedy, the terrible and the ludicrous, are so blended, Napoleon said to Göethe, "I am amazed that a profound intellect such as yours should not prefer the more *distinctly defined forms!*"

Of the Emperor Alexander, Napoleon wrote, "I am pleased with Alexander, as he ought to be with me. If he were a woman I believe I should fall in love with him."

The Marquis of St. Simon, who had taken the oath of fidelity to king Joseph of Spain, was found fighting against his country, and condemned to death. His daughter threw herself at Napoleon's feet as he passed. "Who is this young girl? What does she wish?" Napoleon asked.

"Sire," she replied, "I am the daughter of St. Simon, who is condemned to die this night." Then she fell insensible to the ground.

Napoleon looked at her pityingly for a moment, and then said, "Let the very best care be taken of Mdlle. St. Simon. Tell her that her father is pardoned."

"Those were barbarous times," Napoleon said, "which they have the folly to represent to us as heroic, when the father sacrificed his children, the wife her husband, the subject his sovereign, the soldier his general, and all without shame or disguise! How are times changed now. You have seen emperors and kings in my power, as well as the capitals of their states, and I exacted from them neither ransom nor sacrifice of honours. The world has seen how I treated the emperor of Austria whom I might have imprisoned; and that successor of Leopold and Henry, who is now more than half in my power will not be worse treated on this occasion than on the preceding one, notwithstanding that he has attacked us with so much perfidy."

"Napoleon and Josephine, wishing to visit the western part of France, went to Etampes. Young villagers, headed by the curé of the place came to present their majesties with beautiful roses and excellent grapes. "Nature is blessed in this province," said the emperor to his wife, as he presented the bouquet to her; "take it, madame, and never forget those whom Providence does not forget."

"Providence," said the good curé, "always blesses labouring men, because they accomplish the most important of his laws."

"Behold," said the Emperor to Josephine, after having thanked the good villagers, "here are men who unite flowers and fruits, the useful and the agreeable; they deserve to be happy."

After the battle of Wagram, Napoleon recognized among the dead a colonel who had displeased him. He stopped and looked at his mangled body for a moment, and then said, " I regret not having told him before the battle that I had forgotten everything.

1809. "Josephine, my own good Josephine," Napoleon said to her on the last of November, 1809, "you know how I have loved you. It is to you alone that I owe the only few moments of happiness I have known in the world. Josephine, my destiny is stronger than my will. My dearest affections must yield to the welfare of France."

To the members of the imperial family and the officers of the empire he said, " The political interests of my monarchy and the wishes of my people, which have constantly guided my actions, require that I should transmit to an heir, inheriting my love for the people, the throne on which Providence has placed me. For many years I have lost all hopes of having children by my beloved spouse the Empress Josephine. It is this consideration which induces me to sacrifice the dearest affections of my heart to consult the good of my subjects only, and to desire the dissolution of our marriage. Arrived at the age of forty years, I may reasonably hope to live long enough to rear, in the spirit of my own thoughts and disposition, the children with which it may please Providence to bless me. God knows how much such a determination has cost my heart. But there is no sacrifice too great for my courage, when it is proved to be in the interests of France. Far from having any cause of complaint, I have nothing to say but in praise of the attachment and tenderness of my beloved wife. She has embellished fifteen years of my life, and the remembrance of them will be for ever engraven on my heart. She was crowned by my hand. She shall always retain the rank and title of empress. Above all, let her never doubt my affection, and always regard me as her best and dearest friend."

1810. One day, at Compiègne, the Duke of Gaëta and the Emperor were walking in the park, when the King of Rome appeared, in the arms of his nurse, accompanied by his governess the Countess of Montesquieu. After caressing his son, he walked on, saying to the Duke of Gaëta, "There is a child who would have been far happier to have been born a private individual, with a moderate income. He is destined to bear a heavy burden upon his shoulders."

1812. "I had," said Napoleon, "a secret instinct that Bernadotte was a serpent whom I was nourishing in my bosom."

"Soldiers!" said Napoleon to his troops before Moscow; "Soldiers! the battle is at hand which you have so long desired. Henceforth the victory depends upon yourselves. It has become necessary, and will give you abundance. Conduct yourselves as you did at Austerlitz, Friedland, Witepsk and Smolensk. Let the remotest posterity recount your actions on this day. Let your countrymen say of you all, 'He was in the great battle under the walls of Moscow.'"

"Not even the fictions of the burning of Troy," said Napoleon, "though heightened by all the powers of poetry, could have equalled the reality of the destruction of Moscow."

As Napoleon left Moscow, he said to Mortier, "Pay every attention to the sick and wounded. Sacrifice your baggage, everything to them. Let the wagons be devoted to their use, and, if necessary, your own saddles. This was the course I pursued at Jean d'Acre. The officers will first relinquish their horses, then the sub-officers, and finally the men. Assemble the generals and officers under your command, and make them sensible how necessary, in their circumstances, is humanity. The Romans bestowed civic crowns on those who preserved their citizens. I shall not be less grateful."

When Napoleon received despatches from France, informing him that a false report of his death had occasioned an outbreak, he exclaimed, with deep feeling, in the presence of his generals: "Does my power, then, hang on so slender a thread? Is my tenure of sovereignty so frail that a single person can place it in jeopardy? Truly, my crown is but ill-fitted to my head if, in my very capital, the audacious attempt of two or three adventurers can make it totter. After twelve years of government—after my marriage—after the birth of my son—after my oaths—my death would have again plunged the country into the midst of revolutionary horrors." Napoleon II. was forgotten.

"Moscow," said Napoleon, "had fallen into our power. We had surmounted every obstacle. The conflagration even had in no way lessened the prosperous state of our affairs. But the rigour of the winter induced upon the army the most frightful calamities. In a few nights all was changed. Cruel losses were experienced. They would have broken my heart if, under such circumstances, I had been accessible to any other sentiments than the welfare of my people. I desire peace. It is necessary. On four different occasions, since the rupture of the peace of Amiens, I have solemnly made offer of it to my enemies. But I will never conclude a treaty but on terms honourable and suitable to the grandeur of my empire."

After the intention of Ivan Petrowisk to assassinate Napoleon at Moscow had been discovered, he said to Caulaincourt, "Coulaincourt, my entrance into Moscow has been marked by gloomy presages. Diabolical machinations have been set on foot here. Religious fanaticism has been called into action. It is a powerful and successful engine when exercised over an uncivilized people. In France, if we were to resort to such jugglery, we should be laughed at. In Russia, it raises up devoted assassins. This war resembles no other. At Eylau, at Friedland, we had to contend only with soldiers, here we have to conquer a whole nation." After his interview with the Russian assassin, he walked several times up and down the room, with his head down and his arms crossed on his chest; then stopping short, he exclaimed: "And Murat!—Murat, without awaiting my orders, without seeking any counsel save that of his own wild brain, has thought fit to take the route to Voladimir! Murat is ardent, brilliant in the field of battle. He possesses dauntless courage; but he is totally devoid of judgment. To know when to stop is sometimes the best proof of understanding. Murat has no common sense. This fanfaronade has thrown me into a most embarrassing dilemma. I cannot call him back without proclaiming our weakness, and to send him reinforcements would be to recommence the war."

1813. When Murat deserted Napoleon, the emperor wrote to his sister Caroline, Murat's wife, "Your husband is extremely brave on the field of battle; but out of sight of the enemy he is weaker than a woman. He has no moral courage."

To Murat himself he wrote, "I do not suspect you to be one of those who think that the lion is dead; but if you have counted on this, you will soon discover your error. Since my departure from Wilna, you have done me all the evil you could. Your title of King has turned your brain."

"It is better to have an open enemy than a doubtful ally," he said at St. Cloud; and afterwards, "My greatest fault, perhaps, was not having dethroned the king of Prussia when I could have done it so easily. After Friedland, I could have separated Silesia from Prussia, and abandoned this province to Saxony."

"The system," said Napoleon, "of the enemies of the French revolution is *war to the death.*"

On starting to join his youthful and inexperienced army at Erfurt, "I envy," said Napoleon, "I envy the lot of the meanest peasant in my dominions. At my age he has fulfilled his duties to his country, and he may remain at home, enjoying the society of his wife and children; while I—I must fly to the camp and engage in the strife of war. Such is my fate."

"My good Louise," said Napoleon, at the same time, "is gentle and submissive. I can trust her. Her love and fidelity for me will never fail. In the current of events there may arise circumstances which decide the fate of an empire. In that case, I hope the daughter of the Cæsars will be inspired by the spirit of her grandmother, Maria Theresa."

Of Marshal Bessières, whose loss deeply affected Napoleon, he wrote to the empress, "Bessières is justly entitled to the name of brave and good. He was distinguished alike for his skill, courage, and prudence; for his great experience in directing cavalry movements, his capacity in civil affairs, and his attachment to the emperor. His death on the field of honour is to be envied. It was too sudden to be painful. He left a blameless reputation—the finest heritage he could bequeath to his children. There are few whose loss could have been so sensibly felt. The whole French army shares his majesty's grief on this melancholy occasion."

"In my young soldiers," said Napoleon, "I have found all the valour of my old companions in arms. I have never seen more bravery and devotion during the whole twenty years that I have commanded the French troops. Had the allied sovereigns and their ministers been present on the field of battle, they would have renounced the vain hope of causing the star of France to decline."

On seeing a young Prussian soldier who was pressing his flag to his bosom in the agonies of death, Napoleon said to his officers, "Gentlemen! you see that a soldier has a sentiment approaching idolatry for his flag. It is the object of his worship as a present received from the hands of his mistress. Render funeral honours at once to this young man. *I regret that I do not know his name that I might write to his family.* Do not take away his flag; its silken folds will be an honourable shroud for him."

As Napoleon approached Dresden, he was waited upon by the magistrates who had been treacherous to him and to their king, and had welcomed the allies.

"Who are you?" said Napoleon, severely.

"Members of the municipality," replied the trembling burgomasters.

"Have you bread for my troops?" inquired Napoleon.

"Our resources," they answered, "have been entirely exhausted by the requisitions of the Russians and Prussians."

"Ah!" replied Napoleon, "it is impossible, is it? I know no such word. Get ready bread, meat, and wine. You richly deserve to be treated as a conquered people. But I forgive all, from regard to your king. He is the saviour of your country. You have been already punished by the presence of the Russians and Prussians, and having been governed by Baron Stein."

On being told that a soldier's wound was incurable, "Try," replied Napoleon; "it is always well to lose one less."

After visiting the tomb of Bessières, he remarked, "That in this pilgrimage to the shrine of the illustrious dead, he had experienced strange presentiments, and, as it were, a revelation of his fate. . . . It is well, sometimes, to visit the tomb, there to converse with the dead."

On the morning of the day that Duroc, the Duke of Friuli, died, Napoleon turned to him and said, "Duroc, Fortune is determined to take one of us to-day."

"I know," said Napoleon to the Duke of Gaëta, "that I shall be reproached with having loved war, and sought it through mere ambition. Nevertheless, they will not accuse me of avoiding its fatigues, nor of having fled from its perils. That at least is something. But who, indeed, can hope to obtain justice while living?"

"When, however, I am no more it will be allowed that, situated as I was, menaced incessantly by powerful coalitions roused and supported by England, I had, in the impossibility of avoiding the conflict but two paths open to me—either to wait until the enemy should pass our frontiers, or to prevent this by attacking him in his own territories; I chose that course which would protect our country from the ravages of inevitable war, and which would save it in some degree from the expense. If our contemporaries persist in reproaching me, posterity, I am confident, will do me justice. It will at least be admitted that, in repelling the attacks which we have not provoked, I did but fulfil the obligations which nature imposes, and not the incitements of an insane ambition. The war in Spain, which was not so directly connected with the coalitions provoked by England, may, perhaps, be criticised by those who are ignorant of the position in which we found ourselves in respect to that government. The conduct of the Spanish court, while I was in the heart of Germany, conclusively proved that France could place no dependence on Spain. All who surrounded me, notwithstanding all that may be said to the contrary, were, without exception, of that opinion. Circumstances unparalleled in history, made me take the initiative in that enterprise; an unfortunate event, which augmented the difficulties, increased still more by the shameful and fatal capitulation of Baylen. Nevertheless, it was of extreme importance to withdraw the Peninsula from the influence of England, otherwise our destruction might be secured whenever we should again be called to a distance from home. I was ever hoping that the time would come when, surrendering myself to the employments of peace, I could prove to France that in the cabinet as well as the camp, I lived but for her happiness."

On receiving the news that Austria had declared against him, Napoleon said, "It would be a thousand times better to perish in battle, in the hour of the enemy's triumph, than to submit to the degradation sought to be inflicted on me. Defeat even, attended by noble-minded perseverance, may leave the respect due to adversity. Hence, I prefer to give battle; for should I be conquered, our fate is too intimately blended with the true political interests of the majority of our enemies to allow great advantages to be taken. Should I be victorious I may save all. I have still chances in my favour, and am far from despairing."

To Lord Whitworth, when remonstrating with him against the rupture of the peace of Amiens:

"You well know that in all I have done, it has been my object to complete the execution of the treaties, and to secure the general peace. Now is there, anywhere, a state that I am threatening? Look; seek about. None, as you well know. If you are jealous of my designs upon Egypt, my lord, I will endeavour to satisfy you. I have thought a great deal about Egypt, and I shall still think more if you force me to renew the war; but I will not endanger the peace which we have enjoyed for so short a time, for the sake of reconquering a nation. The Turkish empire threatens to fall. For my part, I shall contribute to uphold it as long as possible. But if it fall to pieces I intend that France shall have her share. But be assured I shall not hasten events. Do you imagine that I deceive myself in regard to the power which I exercise at this moment over France and Europe? Now that power is not great enough to allow me to venture with impunity upon an aggression, without adequate motive. The opinion of Europe would instantly turn against me. My political ascendancy would be lost. And as for France, it is necessary for me to prove to her that war is made upon me, that I have not provoked it, in order to inspire her with that enthusiastic ardour which I purpose to excite against you if you oblige me to fight. *All the faults must be yours, and not one of them mine.* I contemplate, therefore, no aggression. I wanted to establish a barrier against those barbarians, by reestablishing the kingdom of Poland, and putting Poniatowski at the head of it as king, but your imbeciles of ministers would not consent. A hundred years I shall be applauded; and Europe, especially England, will lament that I did not succeed. When they see the finest countries in Europe overcome, and a prey to those northern barbarians, they will say, 'Napoleon was right!'"

At Dresden, Napoleon resolving to disperse a group of horsemen who had come to reconnoitre his position, sent the following order to the captain of the battery, "Throw a dozen bullets at a time into that group, there may be some little generals in it."

"The fate of war," Napoleon said to Murat, "is to be exalted in the morning and low enough at night. There is but one step from triumph to ruin."

Of Poniatowski, who died while crossing the Elster, Napoleon said, "Poniatowski was a noble man, honourable and brave. Had I succeeded in Russia, I intended to make him king of Poland."

"From the moment when we decided on the concentration of power, which could alone save us," said Napoleon, in conversation with Las Cases; "when we determined on the unity of doctrines and resources which rendered us a mighty nation, the destinies of France depended wholly upon the character, the principles and the measures of him who had been invested with the accidental dictatorship. From that moment the *State was myself.* . . . When I said that France stood more in need of me than I of her, this solid truth was declared to be mere excess of vanity. I was myself the keystone of an edifice totally new, and raised on a slight foundation. Its stability depended on each of my battles. . . . The majority blamed my ambition as the cause of these wars. But they were not my choice; they were the results of nature and the force of events."

1814. In a battle with the allies at Montereau, a little town sixty miles south-east of Paris, Napoleon was requested to retire from the field to a place of safety, "Courage, my friends," he said, "the ball which is to kill me is not yet cast."

At the close of the last meeting between Napoleon and Josephine, he took her hand and looking tenderly at her said, "Josephine, I have been as fortunate as any man upon earth. But in this hour, when a storm is gathering over me, I have none but you in the wide world upon whom I can repose."

Speaking with Caulaincourt, years afterwards, of the scenes in Paris in 1814, before the capitulation, he said, "My head burns; I am feverish; if I live a hundred years I shall never forget these scenes. They are the fixed ideas of my sleepless nights. My reminiscences are fearful. They kill me. The rest of the tomb is sweet after such sufferings."

When Caulaincourt informed Napoleon that he was required to surrender the crown of France to his son, he replied, in a terribly impressive tone, "That is to say, they will not treat with me. They mean to drive me from the throne which I conquered by my sword. They wish to make a Helot of me, an object of derision, intended for an example to those who, by their genius and superior talent alone, command men, and make lawful kings tremble on their worm-eaten thrones. . . . When I was happy I thought I knew men, but it was fated that I should know them in misfortune only."

"Restore the Bourbons!" Napoleon exclaimed, in another conversation; "it is not merely madness, but it shows a desire to inflict every kind of misery on the country. Is it true, really, that such an idea is seriously entertained? . . . The Senate cannot surely consent to see a Bourbon on the throne. Setting aside the baseness of agreeing to such an arrangement, what place could be assigned to the Senate in a court from which they or their fathers before them dragged Louis XVI. to the scaffold? As for me, I was a new man, unsullied by the vices of the French revolution. I had no motive for revenge. I had everything to reconstruct. I should never have dared to sit on the vacant throne of France, had not my brow been bound with laurels. The French people elevated me, because I had executed with them, and for them, great and noble works. But the Bourbons! What have they done for France? What proportion of the victories, of the glory, or prosperity of France, belongs to them? Tranquillity will never be insured to the Bourbons in Paris. Remember my prophecy, Caulaincourt."

Napoleon's abdication was contained in the following terms:—

"The allied powers having proclaimed that the Emperor Napoleon was the sole obstacle to the re-establishment of peace, the Emperor Napoleon, faithful to his oath, declares that he is ready to descend from the throne, to quit France, and life itself, for the good of the country; but without prejudice to the rights of his son, to those of the empress as regent, and to the maintenance of the laws of the empire.

"Given at our palace at Fontainebleau, the 4th of April, 1814."

On the 6th of April, this was altered as follows:—
"The allied sovereigns having declared that the Emperor Napoleon is the sole obstacle to the re-establishment of a general peace in Europe, the Emperor Napoleon, faithful to his oath, declares that he renounces, for himself *and his heirs* the throne of France and Italy; and that there is no personal sacrifice, not even that of life itself, which he is not willing to make for the interests of France."

"Caulaincourt," Napoleon said, "this last experience of mankind has irrevocably banished from me those illusions which help to counteract the cares of sovereignty. I have no longer any faith in patriotism: it is a mere empty word expressing a noble idea. The love of country is the love of one's self, of one's position, of one's personal interest . . . Interest! that miserable motive is now paramount over every other in France.

"There is no longer faith or integrity in the bond which unites the nation to its sovereign. France is verging towards her decline. . . . The future is pregnant with disasters. . . . . Kings are treading on volcanic ground. . . . . The Bourbons have stripped from the crown the halo with which I sought to encircle it. . . . How short-sighted. . . . They cannot perceive that by disavowing our glory and our conquests—by depreciating the great and brilliant works which have elevated the throne they are destroying its illusions. I have elevated, not degraded royalty. I have made it great and powerful. I have presented it under a new and favourable aspect, to a people to whom it had become obnoxious—I had collected round the national throne everything that could fix popular admiration. My successors will not feel the value of these attractions. They will imprudently strip off the velvet and gold, and show that the throne is only a few deal planks."

If Caulaincourt is to be credited, Napoleon endeavoured to commit suicide by taking poison, at Fontainebleau, after his abdication. Caulaincourt was called in the middle of the night to see Napoleon, whom he found in a frightfully convulsed condition, attended by Ivan, who was vainly endeavouring to produce vomiting by making his patient take hot tea. Napoleon, however, pushed the cup aside, and said, " I am dying, Caulaincourt—to you I commend my wife and son; defend my memory—I can no longer support life." After again and again refusing the cup, he exclaimed, " Leave me alone! leave me alone!" Finally, Caulaincourt and Ivan prevailed upon him to drink several times, and repeated vomitings brought some relief. During the time that he slept after, Constant told Caulaincourt that he heard a noise in the emperor's chamber, and upon going to him, found him in violent convulsions, with his face buried in the pillow to stifle his cries. Constant called Ivan, whom, when the emperor saw, he said, " Ivan, the dose was not strong enough."

" *Then it was,*" says Caulaincourt, "*that they acquired the sad certainty that he had taken poison.*"

" Suicide," Napoleon said to Caulaincourt, afterwards, " is sometimes committed for love. What folly! Sometimes for the loss of fortune. There it is cowardice. Another cannot live after he has been disgraced. What weakness! But," he concluded, egotistically, " to survive the loss of empire—to be exposed to the insults of one's contemporaries—that is true courage."

"There is something harder to bear than the reverses of fortune," he continued, presently. "Do you know what pierces the heart most deeply? it is the ingratitude of man. I am tired of life. Death is rest. What I have suffered during the last twenty years cannot be understood. . . . Caulaincourt, there have been moments in these last days when I thought I should go mad—when I have felt such a devouring heat here. Madness is the last stage of human degradation. It is the abdication of humanity. Better to die a thousand times. In resigning myself to life, I accept nameless tortures. No matter, I will endure them."

Before his departure for Elba, Napoleon, bidding farewell to his troops, said, "Generals, officers, and soldiers of my Old Guard, I bid you farewell. For five and twenty years I have ever found you in the path of honour and glory. In these last days, as in our days of prosperity, you have never ceased to be models of fidelity and courage. Europe has armed against us. Our cause never could have been lost with such men as you. We could have maintained a civil war for years. But it would have made our country unhappy. I leave you. But, my friends, *be faithful to the new sovereign whom France has accepted.* After embracing General Petit, who commanded the " Old Guard," Napoleon asked for the eagle; when a grenadier advanced with it, he kissed its silver beak, pressed it to his heart, and said, with a faltering voice, "Dear Eagle, may this last embrace vibrate for ever in the hearts of all my faithful soldiers! Farewell once more, my old companions—farewell!"

From Elba, Napoleon wrote to Caulaincourt, "It is less difficult than people think to accustom one's self to a life of retirement and peace, when one possesses within one's self some resource to make time useful. I employ myself much in my study, and when I go out I enjoy some happy moments in seeing again my brave grenadiers. Here my reflections are not continually coming in contact with painful recollections."

Again he wrote: "The lot of a dethroned king, who has been born a king and nothing more, must be dreadful. The pomp of the throne, the gewgaws which surround him from his cradle, and which accompany him step by step throughout his life, become a necessary condition of his existence. For me, always a soldier, and a sovereign by chance, the luxuries of royalty proved a heavy charge. The toils of war and a rough camp life are best suited to my organization, my habits, and my tastes. Of all my past grandeur, I alone regret my soldiers; and of all the jewels of my crown, the French uniforms which they allowed me to take with me are the most precious I have preserved."*

---

* "Methinks
There's something lonely in the state of kings!
None dare come near them. As the eagle, poised
Upon his sightless throne in upper air,
Scares gentler birds away, so kings (cut off
From human kindred, by the curse of power)

E

An American, in "Napoleon his own Historian," gives the following account of an interview with Napoleon, at Elba:—

"You come from France?" he said.

"Yes, sire."

"You must have found Paris extremely embellished?"

"The public monuments are magnificent."

"I had projected many others. My purpose was to spend four hundred millions in doing honour to military courage. Paris would have had temples superior to those of Rome. I hope what I had begun will be continued. I finished the Louvre. The king ought to finish the Temple of Glory. Is the king beloved?"

"Yes, sire."

"He is a man of some talents; I always had a great esteem for him. He has not an easy task to perform; I exhorted my soldiers to be faithful to him. A civil war in France is above all things to be deprecated; it could only take place in my favour. I renounced the throne voluntarily. I would gladly have preserved it for my son; but a regency was very difficult after all that had passed. It could have had no stability but in the case

---

Are shunned and live alone. Who dare come near
The region of a king? There is a wall
(Invisible, indeed, yet strong and high,)
Which fences kings from close approach of men.
They live respected—oh, that cheat, 'respect'!—
As if the homage which abases others
Could comfort him that has 't. Alone—alone!
Prisoned in ermine and a velvet chair,
Shut out from hope (the height being all attained),
Yet touched by terrors,—what can soothe a king?"
BARRY CORNWALL.

of my having fallen in battle.—Did you see the Emperor Alexander?"

"Once, at the theatre."

"He must have been received with acclamations; he has conducted himself very well with regard to the French. He has great qualities, he is good and generous; but these are not sufficient to command; he loses himself in little things. I have been much in the wrong with regard to him. My war was unjust; but I was obliged to undertake it, or give up the continental system.—Is it true that my museum has not been touched?"

"I understood that nothing had been taken away, and that this was entirely owing to the Emperor Alexander."

"Such generosity is admirable; in his place, I should not have been so forbearing; there is true greatness in such a procedure. However, as a man in his situation should always do something extraordinary, he must either take all or leave all; and to take all would perhaps have been difficult with the French. What do they think of the senate in France?"

"The ancient members are not held in much esteem."

"The king ought to discard them all."

Here Napoleon's countenance, which had hitherto been mild and pleasant, assumed an expression of anger. He added, "I wished to preserve my authority only to punish them; those cringing courtiers are guilty of all the ills which I have brought upon France. They never opposed my will; fear of losing their places rendered them more supple and despicable than were the Roman senate under their emperors. Their speakers thought of nothing but inventing new phrases of adulation in addressing me, and approving the wisdom of my decrees.

They were loaded with my favours, and they betrayed me from fear for themselves, not in the idea of saving France. Those wretches are shameless enough to do anything which they think is for their personal interest; they will betray the king as easily as they betrayed me, if they believe that anything is to be gained by it. With the exception of two or three of the ancient military, the king ought to sweep the halls of the Luxembourg free of these reptiles. Their servility made me a despot. If some of the senators had opposed my will, I should have discarded them, 'tis true; but their energy would have saved France from a torrent of evil. I should have been afraid of new opposition, and looked more carefully to what I was about. If they had sometimes opposed me, I should have had less contempt for mankind. I feel that I possess such qualities as might have rendered France happy; but then I ought to have had about me men of some firmness, not so thirsty of favour and fortune. For ten years I found nothing but courtiers, and was surrounded by nothing but flatteries. What man could resist this? I will say confidently, not one. Every year of my reign I saw more and more plainly, that the harsher the treatment men received the greater was their submission and devotion. My despotism then increased in proportion to my contempt for mankind. Those who first shunned places at my court, afterwards were the most forward to solicit them. My antechamber was filled with the ancient French *noblesse;* I saw nothing but *courtiers* around me, not a single *man.* The French, so brave in the field, have no civic courage."

On another occasion, Napoleon said to this same gentleman, "I committed three great political faults. I ought to have made peace with England in abandoning Spain; I ought to have restored the kingdom of Poland, and not have gone to Moscow; I ought to have made peace at Dresden, giving up Hamburgh, and some other countries that were useless to me."

1815. After the battle of Waterloo, the Emperor returned to the Elysée, where Caulaincourt awaited him. "He endeavoured," says Caulaincourt, "to give vent to the emotions of his heart, but his oppressed respiration permitted him to articulate only broken sentences."

"The army," he said, "has performed prodigies of valour . . . inconceivable efforts. . . . What troops! Ney behaved like a madman. . . . He caused my cavalry to be cut to pieces. . . . All has been sacrificed. . . . I am ill and exhausted. . . . I must lie down for an hour or two. . . . My head burns. . . . I must take a bath."

After his bath, "It is grievous," he continued, "to think that we should have been overcome after so many heroic efforts. My most brilliant victories do not shed more glory on the French army than the defeat of Mont St. Jean. . . . Our troops have not been beaten; they have been sacrificed—massacred by overwhelming numbers. . . . My guards suffered themselves to be cut to pieces without asking for quarter. . . . I wished to have died with them, but they exclaimed, 'Withdraw, withdraw, you see that Death is resolved to spare your majesty.' And opening their ranks, my old grenadiers screened me from the carnage, forming around me a rampart of their bodies. . . . My brave, my admirable guard, has been destroyed . . . and I have not perished with them."

"I had," resumed the emperor, "conceived a bold

manœuvre, with the view of preventing the junction of the two hostile armies. I had combined my cavalry into a single corps of twenty thousand men, and ordered it to rush into the midst of the Prussian cantonments. This bold attack, which was executed on the 14th, with the rapidity of lightning, seemed likely to decide the fate of the campaign. French troops never calculate the number of an enemy's force. . . . They care not how they shed their blood in success. . . . They are invincible in prosperity; but I was compelled to change my plan. Instead of making an unexpected attack, I found myself obliged to engage in a regular battle, having opposed to me two combined armies, supported by immense reserves. The enemy's forces quadrupled the number of ours. I had calculated all the disadvantages of a regular battle. The infamous desertion of Bourmont forced me to change all my arrangements. To pass over to the enemy on the eve of a battle! Atrocious! The blood of his fellow-countrymen be on his head! The maledictions of France will pursue him."

"Sire," observed Caulaincourt, "how unfortunate that you did not follow your own impulse; on a former occasion you rejected that man."

"Oh! this baseness is incredible. The annals of the French army offer no precedent for such a crime. Jomini was not a Frenchman. The consequences of this defection have been most disastrous. It has created despondency in the minds of those who witnessed the paralyzing effects of previous treasons. My orders were not properly understood, and consequently there was some degree of hesitation in executing them. At one time Grouchy was too late; at another time, Ney was carried away by his enthusiasm and intrepidity. He exposed himself to danger like any common soldier, without looking either before or behind him; and his troops were sacrificed without any necessity. It is deplorable to think of it! Our army performed prodigies of valour, and yet we have lost the battle. Generals, marshals, all fought gloriously; but, nevertheless, an indescribable uncertainty and anxiety pervaded the commanders of the army. There was no unity, no precision, in the movements—and," he added, with painful emotion, "I have been assured that cries of *Sauve qui peut* were uttered. I cannot believe this. What I suffered, Caulaincourt, was worse than the tortures of Fontainebleau. I feel that I have had my death wound. The blow I received at Waterloo is mortal!"

When Caulaincourt visited Napoleon at Malmaison, he said to him:—

"Well, Caulaincourt! this is truly draining the cup of misfortune to the dregs. I wished to defer my departure only for the sake of fighting at the head of the army. I wished only to contribute my aid in repelling the enemy. I have had enough of sovereignty. I want no more of it, I want no more of it." (He repeated these words with marked vehemence). "I am no longer a sovereign, but I am still a soldier! When I heard the cannon roar—when I reflected that my troops were without a leader—that they were to endure the humiliation of a defeat without having fought—my blood boiled with indignation. All I wished for was a glorious death amidst my brave troops. But my co-operation would have defeated the schemes of traitors, France has been sold. She has been surrendered without a blow being struck in her defence. Thirty-two millions of men have been made to bow their heads to an arrogant conqueror, without disputing the victory. Such a spectacle as France now presents is not to be found in the history of any other nation. What has France become in the hands of the imbecile government which has ruled her for the last fifteen months? Is she any longer the nation unequalled in the world? . . . In 1814, honest men might justly say, all is lost except honour—except national dignity. Let them now bow down their heads with mortification, for now all—all is lost. . . . And that villain Fouché imagines that I would resume the sovereignty in the degradation to which it is now reduced. Never—never. The place that is assigned to the sovereign is no longer tenable. I am disgusted alike with men and things, and I am anxious only to enjoy repose. I am utterly indifferent about my future fate—and I endure life, without attaching myself to it by any alluring chimeras. I carry with me from France recollections which will constitute at once the charm and torment of the remainder of my days. A bitter and incurable regret must ever be connected with this last phase of my singular career. Alas! what will come of the army—my brave, my unparalleled army! The reaction will be terrible, Caulaincourt. The army will be doomed to expiate its fidelity to my cause, its heroic resistance at Waterloo. Waterloo! What horrible recollections are connected with that name! O! if you had seen that handful of heroes, closely pressed one upon another, resisting immense masses of the enemy, not to defend their lives, but to meet death on the field of battle where they could not conquer! The English stood amazed at sight of this desperate heroism, and weary of the carnage, they implored the martyrs to surrender. This merciful summons was answered by the sublime cry, '*Le garde meurt, et ne se rend pas.'* * The Imperial guard has immortalized the French people and the empire!"

When the crowd around the Champs Elysées was tumultuous in its acclamations, Napoleon turned to Benjamin Constant, who had urged him to arm the masses, and said, " These poor people who now come to condole with me in my reverses, I have not loaded with honours and riches. I leave them poor as I found them. But the instinct of country enlightens them. The voice of the nation speaks through their mouths. I have but to utter a word and the Chamber of Deputies would exist no longer. But no! not a single life shall be sacrificed to me. I have not come from Elba to inundate Paris with blood."

One morning, at Paris, while Napoleon was seated in his cabinet, a child entered the room, and presented him coffee and refreshments on a tray. Napoleon did not at first notice his entrance. "Eat, sire," the child at length said, " it will do you good."

The Emperor raised his eyes and said, " You come from the village Gonesse, do you not?"

"No, sire," the child replied, " I come from Pierrefite."

---

* This phrase, attributed to Cambronne, who was made prisoner at Waterloo, he vehemently denied. It was invented by a celebrated inventor of *bon mots*, Rougemont, and appeared in the "Indépandant" two days after the battle. Cambronne, when pressed by a lady to repeat the words he really did use, replied, " Ma foi, Madame, je ne sais pas au juste ce que j'ai dit à l'officier Anglais qui me criait de me rendre : mais ce qui est certain est qu'il comprenait le Français, et qu'il m'a répondu *mange.*"

"Where your parents," Napoleon added, "have a cottage and some acres of land?"

"Yes, sire," the child replied.

"There," exclaimed the Emperor, "is true happiness."

"Frenchmen! In commencing the war for the upholding of national independence, I relied on the union of all efforts and all wills, and upon the concurrence of all the national authorities. I had every reason to expect success, and I brave the declaration of the allies against me. Circumstances appear to me changed. I offer myself in sacrifice to the hatred of the enemies of France. May they prove sincere in their declarations, and hate only my person! My political life is at an end, and I proclaim my son, under the title of Napoleon II. Emperor of the French. The present ministers will provisionally form the council of government. The interest I feel in my son prompts me to request the Chambers to organize, without delay, the regency by a law. Let all unite for the public safety, and to remain an independent nation. NAPOLEON."

"My son will yet reign over France," said Napoleon, "but his time has not yet arrived."

"The English government," said Napoleon to Fleury, "has no magnanimity; the *nation*, however, is great, noble, generous. It will treat me as I ought to be treated. But after all, what can I do? Would you have me allow myself to be taken like a child, by Wellington, to adorn his triumph in London? I have only one course to adopt, that of retiring from the scene. Destiny will do the rest. Certainly I could die. I could say like Hannibal, 'Let me deliver them from the terror with which I inspire them.' But suicides must be left to weak heads and souls badly tempered. As for me, whatever may be my destiny, I shall not hasten my natural end by a single moment."

On board the Bellerophon, Napoleon said, "What I most admire is the silence and orderly conduct of the men. On board a French ship, every one calls out and gives orders, gabbling like so many geese."

On his first introduction to the Briars, and Mr. and Mrs. Balcombe, who lived there, he found their two daughters, aged respectively thirteen and fifteen years, taking a lesson in geography. He sat down at the table with them and began talking gaily to them. He took up a book and asked the younger child, "Do you learn geography?"

"Yes," she answered, "it is very tiresome, but mamma wishes it."

"You must obey your parents," said the Emperor. "Do you know your Capitals?"

"Oh yes. I have just learnt them."

"And what is the Capital of Russia?" asked the Emperor.

She blushed a little, and answered, "It was Moscow, *once*."

"Why once?" proceeded her questioner.

"Because it is St. Petersburgh now."

"And why so?"

She blushed still more, and answered, after a little hesitation, "Because Moscow is burnt."

"And who burnt it?"

This question completely disconcerted her, she looked down and murmured that she did not know. General Bertrand burst into a long laugh. The Emperor laughed also, and said:

"See how they teach children! I am certain that in this book, which I cannot read, (it was in English) I am represented burning Moscow, as Nero burnt Rome."

"The idea of imprisonment at St. Helena is perfectly horrible. To be enchained for life on an island within the tropics, at an immense distance from any land, cut off from all communication with the world, and everything it contains that is dear to me. It is worse than Tamerlane's iron cage. I would prefer being delivered up to the Bourbons. They style me *General!* They might as well call me *Archbishop.* I was head of the Church as well as of the army. Had they confined me in the Tower of London, or in one of the fortresses of England, though not what I had hoped from the generosity of the English people, I should not have had so much cause for complaint. But to banish me to an island within the tropics! They might as well sign my death-warrant at once. It is impossible that a man of my habit of body can exist long in such a climate."

"Occupation is the scythe of time," Napoleon said to Las Cases. "A man must fulfil his destinies. This is my grand doctrine. Very well! Let mine be accomplished."

Napoleon wrote the following protest from the Bellerophon, August 4th, 1815:

"I hereby solemnly protest in the face of Heaven and mankind, against the violence that is done me, and the violation of my most sacred rights, in disposing of my person and liberty. I voluntarily came on board the Bellerophon; I am not the prisoner, I am the guest of England.

I came at the instigation of the captain himself, who said he had orders from the government to receive and convey me to England, together with my suite, if agreeable to me. I came forward with confidence to place myself under the protection of the laws of England. Once on board the Bellerophon, I was entitled to the hospitality of the British people. If the government, in giving the captain of the Bellerophon orders to receive me, only wished to lay a snare, it has forfeited its honour and disgraced its flag. If this act be consummated, it will be in vain for the English to talk henceforth of their sincerity, their laws, and liberties. British faith will have been lost in the hospitality of the Bellerophon. I appeal to history. It will say that an enemy, who made war for twenty years against the English people, came spontaneously, in the hour of misfortune, to seek an asylum under their laws. What more striking proof could he give of his esteem and confidence? But how did England reply to such an act of magnanimity? It pretended to hold out a hospitable hand to the enemy, and on giving himself up with confidence, he was immolated.

"NAPOLEON."

"They may call me what they please; they cannot prevent me from being *myself*."

As the Northumberland passed France on its way to St. Helena, Napoleon uncovered his head, bowed to the distant hills, and 'said, with deep emotion, " Land of the brave, I salute thee! Farewell! France, farewell!"

1816. Napoleon hated flogging. "I raised many thousands of Italians," said he, "who fought with a bravery equal to that of the French, and who did not desert me in danger. What was the cause? I abolished flogging. Instead of the lash I introduced the stimulus of honour. Whatever debases a man cannot be serviceable. What sense of honour can a man have who is flogged before his comrades? When a soldier has been debased by stripes he cares little for his own reputation, or the honour of his country. After an action, I assembled the officers and soldiers, and inquired who had proved themselves heroes. Such as were able to read and write I promoted. Those who were not I ordered to study five hours a day, until they had learned a sufficiency, and then promoted them. Thus I substituted honour and emulation for terror and the lash."

Napoleon was a fatalist.[*] He never feared death, because he believed he should not die until his appointed time came.

"I am," said he, "the creature of circumstances. I do but go where events point out the way. I do not give myself any uneasiness about death. When a man's time is come he must go."

"Are you a Predestinarian?" inquired O'Meara.

"As much so as the Turks are," Napoleon replied. "I have been always so. When destiny wills it must be obeyed. I will give you an example. At the siege of Toulon I noticed an officer who was very careful of

---

[*] He was such a firm believer in fate, that it is said he continually carried about with him and consulted a "Book of Fate," translated by his orders from a MS. 'he met with in Egypt.

himself, instead of showing a courageous example to his men. 'Mr. Officer,' said I, 'come out and observe the effect of your shot. You know not whether your guns are well directed or not.' Very reluctantly he came outside the parapet to the place where I was standing. Wishing to expose as little of his body as possible, he stooped down and partially sheltered himself behind the parapet, and looked under my arm. Just then a shot came close to me, low down, and knocked him to pieces. Now if this man had stood upright he would have been safe, as the ball would have passed between us, and hurt neither." *

One day, Napoleon, conversing with Las Cases, asked him, "Were you a gamester?"

"Alas, sire," Las Cases replied, "I must confess that I was, but only occasionally."

"I am glad," replied Napoleon, "that I knew nothing of it at the time. You would have been ruined in my esteem. A gamester was sure to lose my confidence. I placed no more trust in him."

---

* "Madame de Bourrienne's account of this is far from charming. According to her account the young officer in question had been recently married, and his young wife with tears had entreated Napoleon to dispense with his services on that day. "The general," says Madame de Bourrienne, "was inexorable, as he himself told us with savage exultation. The young officer appears to have had a presentiment of his fate. He was stationed beside the general, and Bonaparte called out to him, ' Take care, there is a bomb shell coming.' Instead of moving to one side the officer stooped, and was cut completely in two. "Bonaparte," concludes Madame de Bourrienne, "laughed loudly while he described the event with horrible minuteness."

Some one read an account of the battle of Lodi, in which it was stated that Napoleon crossed the bridge first, and that Lannes passed after him.

"Before me! before me!" Napoleon exclaimed. "Lannes passed first, I only followed him. I must correct that error on the spot."

Napoleon's handwriting was of a most unintelligible character.

"Do you write orthographically?" he asked his amanuensis one day at St. Helena. "A man occupied with public business cannot attend to orthography. His ideas must flow faster than his hand can trace. He has only time to place his points. He must compress words into letters, and phrases into words, and let the scribes make it out afterwards."

"The rapid succession of your victories," said Las Cases to Napoleon, "must have been a source of great delight to you."

"By no means," Napoleon replied; "those who think so know nothing of the peril of our situation. The victory of to-day was instantly forgotten in preparation for the battle which was to be fought on the morrow. The aspect of danger was continually before me. I enjoyed not one moment of repose."

"Tents," said Napoleon, "are unhealthy; it is much better for the soldier to bivouac in the open air, for then he can build a fire and sleep with warm feet. Tents are necessary only for the general officers, who are obliged to read and consult their maps."

At St. Helena, when Napoleon had time to remember his early youth, he said to Montholon :—

"What recollections of childhood crowd upon my memory. I am carried back to my first impressions of the life of man. It seems to me always, in these moments of calm, that I should have been the happiest man in the world with an income of twenty-five hundred dollars a year, living as the father of a family with my wife and son, in our old house at Ajaccio . . . I still remember with emotion the most minute details of a journey in which I accompanied Paoli. More than five hundred of us, young persons of the first families in the island, formed his body guard. I felt proud of walking by his side, and he appeared to take pleasure in pointing out to me the passes of our mountains which had been witnesses of the heroic struggle of our countrymen for independence. The impression made upon me still vibrates in my heart. . . . Religion is the dominion of the soul. It is the hope of life, the anchor of safety, the deliverance from evil. What a service has Christianity rendered to humanity! what a power would it still have did its ministers comprehend their mission!"

To Las Cases Napoleon said, after reading an account of his sayings, in which the writer had made him speak with too much goodness. "What is popularity? Who was more popular than the unfortunate Louis XVI? Nevertheless, what was his fate? He has perished. One must determine to serve the people and not please them; the best way to gain them is to do them good; nothing is more dangerous than to flatter them; if they do not have all they want afterwards they fret themselves and think you have broken your word to them. The first duty of a prince, undoubtedly, is to do what the people wish, but the people do not always wish what they say they do; their will, their wants should be found not so much in the mouth as in the heart of the prince.

"All systems can doubtless maintain themselves, that of complaisance as well as that of severity; each has its advantages and its inconveniences; everything is equal in this world. If you ask me what my severe expressions have saved me from, I answer, They have spared me from doing what I threatened. What wrong, after all, have I done? What blood have I shed? Who can boast that he would have done better, in the circumstances in which I was placed? What period of history, with similar results to mine, shows such innocent results? For what do they reproach me? They have seized the records of my administration, they have remained masters of my papers, and what have they brought to light? All sovereigns in my position, in the midst of factions, troubles, and conspiracies, are surrounded with murders and executions, are they not? Yet see the sudden calm of France under me."

After dinner, says Las Cases, he turned to me and said suddenly, "Where do you think Madame Las Cases is at this moment?"

"Alas, sire," I answered, "God knows."

"She is at Paris," he continued, "to-day is Tuesday, it is nine o'clock, she is at the Opera."

"No, sire," I replied, "she is too good a woman to go sight-seeing while I am here."

"Just like husbands," said Napoleon, laughing, "always confident and credulous."

Then he turned to General Gourgaud and teased him in the same way about his mother and sister. Gourgaud became sad, and the tears sprung to his eyes. Napoleon looking round at him, said, in a charming manner, "Is it not wicked of me, very barbarous, very tyrannical, to touch such tender chords thus?"

"Poor France," said Napoleon, "what will be thy destiny? What has become of thy glory? What will be thy hopes, thy resources? A king without system, uncertain, using half-measures, when they should be positive and extreme; a shade of ministry when so much force and talent is required, division in the royal house when unanimity is necessary; a prince of the blood at the head of a wholly national opposition. What subjects for troubles, what combinations for the future, who can guess the *dénouement?* . . . Louis XVIII. last year could identify himself with the nation, now he has no choice, he must adopt the principles of his party, he can no longer use any but the *régime* of his fathers. On the other side the allies have not better understood their interests; it was necessary to weaken France, but not to drive it to desperation, it was necessary to take territory from it, but not to impose contributions upon it. That is not the way to treat twenty-eight millions of men. The French, at least, ought to repurchase the loss of glory by peace and happiness. In imposing humiliations, bread must be given; it was necessary to try to reduce this great body to stagnation."

Colonel Wilks, remarking to Napoleon that almost every soldier in the French army showed the germs of an officer, he replied:—

"That is one of the great consequences of the conscription; it made the French army superior to any of its predecessors. It was," he continued, "an institution eminently national, and already far advanced in our manners; the mothers only were afflicted by it, and the time should have come when a girl would not have cared for a man who was not willing to pay his debt to his country. And it is in this state alone," added he, " that the conscription would have acquired the last measure of its advantages, when it has become no longer a constraint and a task, but a point of honour of which every one is jealous; then only a nation is grand and glorious and strong; then its existence can defy reverses, invasions, and time.

"Finally," he continued, " it is true that there is nothing the French will not do at the appearance of danger, it seems to give them spirit, it is their Gallic heritage. Valour, and a love of glory are an instinct with the French, a sort of sixth sense. How many times in the heat of battles I have stopped to look at my young conscripts throwing themselves into the thick of the fight for the first time, honour and courage coming from all their pores."

Napoleon was not at all satisfied with the histories of France, " Velly," he said, "was full of words and empty of things, and those who continued his work are still worse." He knew Garnier, who lived near Malmaison, and to whom he granted a pension. " I believe," said the Emperor, "that the good man, in his gratitude, would at that instant have written willingly and from the bottom of his heart, whatever one had wished."

" At Marengo," said Napoleon, "the Austrians were beaten most thoroughly; their troops behaved admirably, but their valour was buried there; we have not discovered them since."

Of the character of Duroc, Napoleon said, "He had strong, tender, and secret passions, of which his cold exterior gave little promise. I was a long time before I knew him, his service was so exact and regular; it was only when my day was entirely finished, and when I was already reposing, that his commenced. Only chance or accident could have made me know him. Duroc was pure and moral, entirely disinterested in receiving, extremely generous in giving."

"The rock of St. Helena," said Napoleon, "is barren and wild, and the climate is monotonous and unhealthy, but the temperature, we must agree, is mild."

"The isle of Elba, considered so wretched a year ago, is a delectable place compared with St. Helena. As to St. Helena, ah! it can defy all regrets to come."

"Tragedy warms the soul, elevates the heart, can and ought to create heroes. In this sense, perhaps, France owes a part of her great actions to Corneille."

To Las Cases, speaking of the invasion of England, he said one day, "I possessed the best army that ever was, that of Austerlitz, that is saying everything. Four days would have sufficed to find me in London; I should not have gone as a conqueror, but a liberator. I should have re-called William III., but with more generosity and disinterestedness. The discipline of my army would have been perfect; it should have been conducted in London as if still at Paris; no sacrifices, not even contributions exacted from the English; we would not have presented ourselves to them as conquerors, but as brothers who came to restore them to their liberty and their rights. I would have told them to assemble and work themselves for their regeneration, that they were our elders in point of political legislation, that we were there for nothing but to enjoy their happiness and their prosperity, and I would have kept strict faith with them. Thus, after the lapse of a few months, these two nations, once so violently antagonistic, would have been composed of people identical, henceforth, by their principles, their maxims, and their interests; and I should have set out thence to work in the middle and north of Europe under the republican colours (I was then first consul) European regeneration, as later I was on the point of working my way from the north to the middle, under monarchical forms. And these two systems might have been both equally good, because they both tended to the same end and would both have been conducted with firmness, moderation, and good faith. What ills that are known to us, and what ills that we are still ignorant of, might poor Europe not have been spared! Never was a project, so great in the interests of civilization, conceived with more generous intentions, and never did one approach nearer its execution. And a remarkable thing, the obstacles which checked me did not come from man; they all came from the elements. In the middle of Europe the sea lost me, and the burning of Moscow, and the ice and snow of winter, frustrated my plans in the north: thus water, air, and fire, all *nature*, and nothing but nature, have been the enemies of a universal regeneration, commanded by nature herself . . . The problems of Providence are insoluble."

After some moments of silence he again continued:

"They thought my invasion was only a vain threat, because they saw no reasonable means for attempting it, but I should have withdrawn, and worked without being seen. I had scattered all our vessels; the English were obliged to run after them to different parts of the world;

our own, at the same time, had nothing to do but return all at once to assemble *en masse* round our coasts. I ought to have seventy or eighty French or Spanish vessels in the channel. I had calculated that I should remain master of it for two months; I had three or four thousand little ships which only awaited the signal; my hundred thousand men went through the manœuvre of embarkation and disembarkation daily as usual; they were full of ardour and good-will, the enterprise was very popular amongst the French, and we were called by the wishes of a great part of England. If my plan worked satisfactorily, one pitched battle should have been sufficient; the issue could not have been doubtful, victory would have placed us in London, and my conduct would have done the rest. The English people trembled under the yoke of the oligarchy . . . we should have presented ourselves with the magic words of equality and fraternity."

"How many superior men are children more than once in a day!"

Napoleon declaimed against temper in women. "Nothing," said he, "announces rank, education, and good breeding in them more than the evenness of their disposition and the desire to please." He said that they were brought up to be mistresses of themselves. "My two wives were always thus; they were certainly very different in their qualities and dispositions, although they were exactly alike on this point. I have never been a witness to the bad humour of one or the other; both were constantly occupied in pleasing me. . ."

Some one remarked that Marie Louise had boasted, that whenever she wanted anything, no matter how difficult it might be to obtain it, she had only to cry for it. The Emperor laughed and said, "That is quite a discovery to me; one might have suspected Josephine of such a thing, but not Marie Louise."

In a moonlight walk with Las Cases, Napoleon said that he had had "the closest acquaintance with two directly different women in his life: one represented art and the graces; the other innocence and simple nature; and both," he observed, "were very worthy. In no one moment of her life did the first adopt attitudes and positions that were not agreeable and seductive; all that art could lavish on attractions was employed by her, but with such skill that it was not perceived. The other, on the contrary, never saw anything to be gained by innocent artifices. The first never asked her husband for anything, but was in debt everywhere; the second did not hesitate to ask when she wanted anything, which was rarely; she would have thought it impossible to get anything without paying for it immediately. For the rest both were good, kind, and much attached to their husband."

"Whoever had known them," says Las Cases, "must have recognized his two empresses."

Speaking to Las Cases of *La Nouvelle Heloise*, that he was reading, he said, "Jean-Jacques has overloaded his subject. He has depicted frenzy. Love should be a pleasure, not a torment."

Las Cases affirmed that there was nothing in Jean-Jacques that a man might not feel.

"I see," said the Emperor, laughing, "that you have given yourself up to the romantic."

Napoleon finally concluded, that "perfect love was ideal happiness; that both were equally visionary, fugitive, mysterious, and inexplicable; and that love, in short, should be the *occupation* of the idle man, the *distraction* of the warrior, the *rock* of the sovereign."

"My one code," said Napoleon, "by its simplicity, has done more good in France than the mass of all the laws that preceded me. Under my reign, crimes were rapidly decreasing; whilst among our neighbours, the English, they increased, on the contrary, in a frightful manner. And that is enough to pronounce definitely upon the respective administrations.[1]

"And see in the United States how, without effort, everything prospers, how happy and peaceful everything is there; it is in reality the public will and interests which govern there. Put the same government at war with the will, the interests of all, and you will immediately see what confusion and what increase of crimes would ensue. Arrived at power, they would have had me a Washington; the words cost nothing, and surely those who said them with such facility did so without knowing either times or places, or men, or things. If I had been in America I would willingly have been a Washington, and I should have had but little merit; for I do not see how it would have been reasonably possible

---

[1] Montvérau ("Situation de l'Angleterre") gives the following table, which bears out Napoleon's words:—

| France. | | | England. | |
Inhabitants.	Condemned to death.	In	Inhabitants.	Condemned to death.
34,000,000	882	1801	16,000,000	3400
42,000,000	392	1811	17,000,000	6400

to do otherwise. . . . For me I could be nothing but a *crowned Washington*. It was not that in a congress of kings, in the midst of kings conquered or mastered, that I could become so. Then and there alone I could show with effect, his moderation, his sagacity, his wisdom; I could not reasonably reach that but through the *universal dictatorship*. I aspired to it. Do they make me a criminal for that? Will they think it was above human powers, *de s'en demettre?* Sylla, gorged with crimes, has dared to abdicate, pursued by public execration. What motive would have had power to stop me? I, who had none but blessings to receive. But to ask of me, before the time, what was not seasonable, was a vulgar folly; for me to announce it, to promise it, would have been taken for verbiage, for charlatanism; it was not my way. . . . I repeat it, it was necessary for me to conquer at Moscow."

The household at Longwood was not always so unanimous as Napoleon liked. On one occasion, he said to them, "You have followed me to be agreeable, you say? *Be brothers!* otherwise you are nothing but troubles to me. *Be brothers!* otherwise you are only a burden to me.

"You talk of fighting, and that under my very eyes! Am I no longer, then, the object of your care, and is not the eye of the stranger still upon us? I wish every one here to be animated with my spirit. . . . I wish all around me to be happy, and I wish all to share in the few enjoyments that are left to us."

One day, Napoleon said, "I could have shared the Turkish empire with Russia; we have discussed the question more than once. Constantinople always saved it. This capital was the great embarrassment, the true stumbling-block. Russia wanted it, and I would not grant it. It is too precious a key; it alone is worth an empire; whoever possesses it can govern the world."

"Talleyrand," said Napoleon to Las Cases, "was always in a state of treason; but it was complicity with fortune. His circumspection was extreme, conducting himself with his friends as if they were his enemies; and with his enemies as if they might become his friends. In the affair of the divorce, he was for the Empress Josephine. It was he who hastened on the war with Spain, although in public he had the art to appear opposed to it. Finally," continued Napoleon, "it was he who was the active cause, and the principal instrument, in the death of the Duke d'Enghien."

"Madame de Maintenon's style charms me," said Napoleon; "if I am deeply wounded by what is bad, I have a feeling, an irresistible attraction, for what is good."

Of Madame de Sevigné, he added, "Her style is undoubtedly full of charm; but you gain nothing by reading her. It is like eating snowballs, with which one can surfeit one's self without satisfying the stomach."

On the 10th of November, while he was walking with Las Cases, he met Mrs. Balcombe, and Mrs. Stuart, a lady on her voyage from England to Bombay. Whilst talking, some slaves toiled up the narrow path with burdens. Mrs. Balcombe, in a rather angry tone, ordered them to keep back; but the Emperor, making room for the slaves, turned to Mrs. Balcombe, and said, mildly, "Respect the burden, madam!"

In conversation with Mr. Balcombe, Napoleon remarked, "I have no faith in medicines. My remedies are fasting and the warm bath. At the same time, I have a higher opinion of the medical, or rather the surgical profession, than of any other. The practice of the law is too severe an ordeal for poor human nature. . . . The man who habituates himself to the distortion of truth, and to exultation at the success of injustice, will, at last, hardly know right from wrong. So with politics, a man must have a conventional conscience. The ecclesiastics become hypocrites, since too much is expected of them. As to soldiers, they are cut-throats and robbers. But the mission of surgeons is to benefit mankind, not to destroy them or to inflame them against each other."

"We are but a handful in one corner of the world," said Napoleon.

Napoleon often received touching testimonials to the admiration, and even affection, that many strangers had for him. On one occasion he said to Las Cases, "See the effect of imagination! How powerful is its influence! Here are people who do not know me, perhaps have never seen me; they have only heard me spoken of, and what do they not feel? What would they not do to serve me? And the same caprice is found in all countries, in all ages, and in both sexes. Yes, imagination rules the world."

One day when the Emperor was not well, "What a miserable thing is man!" said he; "the smallest fibre in his body, assailed by disease, is sufficient to derange his whole system. On the other hand, in spite of all the maladies to which he is subject, it is sometimes necessary to employ the executioner to put an end to him. What a curious machine is this earthly clothing! And perhaps I may be confined in it for thirty years longer."

Some one remarked to Napoleon that the clouds of detraction would disperse as his memory advanced in posterity.

"That is true," he replied, "and my fate may be said to be the very opposite of others. A fall usually has the effect of lowering a man's character. But on the contrary, my fall has elevated me prodigiously. Every succeeding day divests me of some portion of my *tyrant's skin.*"

O'Meara asked Napoleon why he had protected the Jews so much.

"I wished them to give up usury," Napoleon answered, "and become like other men. They were very numerous in the countries over which I reigned; I hoped, by making them free, and giving them equal rights with Catholics, Protestants, and others, to make them good citizens, and force them to conduct themselves like the rest of the world. . . . My system was to make no religion predominant, but to allow perfect liberty of conscience and thought, to make all men equal, Catholics, Protestants, Mahometans, deists, or others; so that their religion might have no influence in obtaining them employments under government, so that it might not make them either sought for or dreaded."

O'Meara once endeavoured to persuade Bonaparte to take some medicine. He refused, and raising his eyes to heaven, said, "That which is written is written. Our days are numbered."

"What," said Napoleon to Las Cases, "what is more overbearing than weakness which feels itself protected by strength? Look at women, for example!"

Napoleon said to Montholon, "I know men, and I tell you that Jesus Christ is not a man! The religion of Christ is a mystery which subsists by its own force, and proceeds from a mind which is not a human mind. We find in it a marked individuality, which originated a train of words and maxims unknown before. Jesus borrowed nothing from our knowledge. He exhibited Himself the perfect example of His precepts. Jesus is not a philosopher; for His proofs are His miracles, and from the first His disciples adored Him. Learning and philosophy are of no use to salvation; and Jesus came into the world to reveal the mysteries of heaven and the laws of the spirit. Alexander, Cæsar, Charlemagne, and myself have founded empires. But upon what did we rest the creations of our genius? Upon *force!* Jesus Christ alone, founded His empire upon love; and at this moment millions of men would die for Him. I die before my time, and my body will be given back to earth, to become food for worms. Such is the fate of him who has been called the Great Napoleon. What an abyss between my deep misery and the eternal kingdom of Christ, which is proclaimed, loved, and adored, and which is extended over the whole earth! Call you this dying? Is it not living rather? The death of Christ is the death of a God!"

"I fear nothing for my renown," Napoleon said at St. Helena. "Posterity will do me justice. It will compare the good I have done with the faults I have committed. If I had succeeded, I should have died with the reputation of being the greatest man who ever lived. From being nothing, I became, by my own exertions, the most powerful monarch in the world, without committing any crime. My ambition was great, but it rested on the opinion of the masses. I have always thought that sovereignty resides in the people. The empire, as I organized it, was but a great republic. Called to the throne by the voice of the people, my maxim has always been, *a career open to talent without distinction of birth.* It is this system of equality for which the European oligarchy detests me. And yet in England, talent and great services raise a man to the highest rank. England should have understood me."

Napoleon uttered the following graphic eulogium upon his family. " What family, in similar circumstances, would have acted better than mine has done ? Every one is not qualified to be a statesman. That requires a combination of powers which does not often fall to the lot of any one. In this respect all my brothers and sisters were singularly situated; they possessed at once too much and too little talent. They felt themselves too strong to resign themselves blindly to a guiding counsellor, and yet too weak to be left entirely to themselves.

" England is said to traffic in everything. Why then does she not sell liberty, for which she might get a high price, and without any fear of exhausting her stock? For example, what would not the poor Spaniards give her to free them from the yoke to which they have again been subjected? I am confident that they would willingly pay any price to regain their freedom. It was I who inspired them with this sentiment, and the error into which I fell might at least be turned into good account by another government. As to the Italians, I have planted in their hearts principles which can never be rooted out. What can England do better than promote and assist the noble impulses of modern regeneration? Sooner or later this regeneration must be accomplished. Sovereigns and old aristocratic institutions may exert their efforts to oppose it, but in vain. They are dooming themselves to the punishment of Josephus. Sooner or later some arm will tire of resistance, and then the whole system will fall to nothing. Would it not be better to yield with a good grace? This was my intention. Why does England refuse to avail herself of the glory and advantage she might derive from this course of proceeding?"

"Shortly after my return from the conquest of Italy," Napoleon said, "I was accosted by Madame de Staël, at a grand entertainment given by M. Talleyrand. She asked me in the midst of a large circle who was the greatest woman in the world. I looked at her and coldly replied, 'She, madame, who has borne the greatest number of children.' Madame de Staël was a little disconcerted at first; she endeavoured to recover herself by observing that it was reported that I was not very fond of women. 'Pardon me, madame,' I replied, 'I am very fond of my wife.' I cannot call her a *wicked* woman; but she was a restless intriguer, possessed of considerable talent and influence."

"All the Emperor Alexander's thoughts," said Napoleon at St. Helena, "are directed to the conquest of Turkey. We have had many discussions about it. At first, his proposals pleased me, because I thought it would enlighten the world, to drive these brutes the Turks out of Europe. But when I reflected upon its consequences, and saw what a tremendous weight of power it would give to Russia, on account of the number of Greeks in the Turkish dominion, who would naturally join the Russians, I refused to consent to it, especially as Alexander wanted Constantinople, which I would not consent to, as it would destroy the equilibrium of power in Europe."

"An aristocracy is the true, the only support of a monarchy," said Napoleon. "Without it the State is a vessel without a rudder—a balloon in the air. A true aristocracy, however, must be ancient. Therein consists its real force, its talismanic charm. That was the only thing which I could not create. Reasonable democracy will never aspire to anything more than obtaining an equal power of elevation to all. The true policy in these times was to employ the remains of the aristocracy with the forms and the spirit of democracy."

"It was the subject of my perpetual dreams," said Napoleon, "to render Paris the real capital of Europe. I sometimes wished it, for instance, to become a city with a population of two, three, or four millions—in a word, something fabulous, colossal, unexampled, until our days, and with establishments suitable to its population."

Speaking of Lannes, Napoleon said: "He would hear of none but me. Undoubtedly he loved his wife and children better, yet he spoke not of them. He was their protector, I his. I was to him something vague and undefined, a superior being, a providence whom he implored. He was a man on whom I could implicitly rely. Sometimes, from the impetuosity of his disposition, he allowed a hasty expression about me to escape him; but he would have blown out the brains of any one who should have ventured to repeat it. Originally, his bodily courage was greater than his judgment, but the latter daily improved; and at the period of his death, he had reached the highest point of his profession, and was a most able commander. I found him a dwarf, and lost him a giant. Had he lived to see our reverses, it would have been impossible for him to have swerved from the path of duty and honour; and he alone was capable, by his own weight and influence, of changing the entire aspect of affairs."

"If I had not conquered at Austerlitz," said Napoleon, "I should have had all Prussia on me. If I had not been victorious at Jena, Austria and Spain would have attacked me in the rear. If I had not triumphed at Wagram—which, by-the-bye, was not so decisive a victory—I had to fear that Russia would abandon me, that Prussia would rise against me; and, in the meantime, the English were already before Antwerp."

"My divorce has no parallel in history. It did not destroy the ties which united our families, and our mutual tenderness remained unchanged. Our separation was a sacrifice demanded of us by reason for the interests of my crown and my dynasty. Josephine was devoted to me. She loved me tenderly. No one ever had a preference over me in her heart. I occupied the first place in it, her children the next. She was right in thus loving me, and the remembrance of her is still all-powerful in my mind."

"Louis," said Napoleon, of his brother, "had been spoilt by reading Rousseau's works. He contrived to agree with his wife only for a few months. There were faults on both sides. On the one hand Louis was too teasing in his temper, and on the other, Hortense was too volatile. They were attached to each other at the time of their marriage, which was agreeable to their mutual wishes. The union was, however, contrived by Josephine, who had her own views in promoting it. I, on the contrary, would rather have extended my connection with other families; and, for a moment, I had an idea of forming a union between Louis and a niece of Talleyrand, who afterward became Madame Juste de Noaille."

Speaking of the proposed surrender of Illyria and Venetian Lombardy to Austria, Napoleon said: "How greatly was I perplexed, to find that I was the only man who could judge of our danger! On the one hand I was disturbed by the coalesced powers, which threatened our very existence; and on the other by my own subjects, who, in their blindness, seemed to make common cause with the foe. Our enemies laboured for my destruction, and the importunities of my ministers and people tended to induce me to throw myself on the mercy of foreigners. I saw that the destinies and principles of France depended upon me alone. The circumstances in which the country was placed were extraordinary and entirely new. It would be vain to seek for a parallel to them. The stability of the edifice of which I was the keystone but depended upon each of my battles. Had I been conquered at Marengo, France would have encountered all the disasters of 1814 and 1815, without those prodigies of glory which succeeded, and which will be immortal.

At Austerlitz, at Jena, at Eylau, and at Wagram, it was the same. The vulgar failed not to blame my ambition as the cause of these wars, but they were not of my choosing. They were caused by the nature and force of events. They arose out of that conflict of the past and the future, that permanent coalition of our enemies which compelled us to subdue, under pain of being subdued."

Once, at St. Helena, when Montholon was going into the town on business, Bonaparte said to him: "Now, Montholon, mind you bring me *no lies* as news, as Marshal Bertrand goes to town to-morrow, and I shall then hear the *truth*."

Napoleon was much insulted at the early and unceremonious visit paid him by Sir George Cockburn and Sir Hudson Lowe, for the purpose of introducing the latter to him as the new Governor of St. Helena.

"The first insult he offered me," said Napoleon, "was at his own table in the Northumberland, shortly after I came on board. I did not wish to sit at table for two or three hours, like the English, guzzling and drinking, and I therefore got up and walked the deck, upon which he said, in a contemptuous manner, 'I believe the General has never read Lord Chesterfield,' meaning that I was deficient in politeness, and did not know how to sit at table; upon which Madame Bertrand, who understands English, said to him, 'Sir, the greatest sovereigns in Europe have thought it an honour to dine with the Emperor Napoleon.' This was a most gross insult to me. I never shall see him with pleasure: my communication with him is finished now. . . . If he wanted to see Lord Keith, or Lord St. Vincent, or Lord Melville, he would have sent to know what time was convenient to them, would he not? and I think the actions I have performed are at least as well known as any the two first have done, setting aside the fact of my having been a crowned head. He is a fool," he continued, " a coarse man."

Napoleon dictated the following for his domestics, who wished to remain with him at Longwood, to sign:—

" We, the undersigned, wishing to continue in the service of H. M. the Emperor Napoleon, consent, horrible as is the abode in St. Helena, to remain here. We submit to the restrictions, though unjust and arbitrary, that are imposed upon H. M. and upon the persons in his service."

" There," said he, when he had finished his dictation, " let those who like sign that."

At Sir Hudson Lowe's second interview with Napoleon, the latter said to him, " The allies have made a convention declaring me their prisoner. What do they mean? They have no authority to do so. I wish you to write to your Government, and acquaint it I shall protest against it. I gave myself up to *England*, and to no other power. It is an act of the British Parliament alone which can warrant such proceedings against me. I have been treated in a cruel manner. I misunderstood the character of the English people. I should have surrendered myself to the Emperor of Russia, who was my friend, or to the Emperor of Austria, who was related to me. There is courage in putting a man to death, but it is an act of cowardice to let him languish, and to poison him in so horrid an island and so detestable a climate. Let them send me a coffin," he continued, presently; " a couple of balls in the head would be quite sufficient.

What does it signify to me whether I lie on a velvet or a fustian couch? I am a soldier and used to everything. I have been landed here like a convict, and proclamations forbid the inhabitants to speak to me."

Apropos of this interview, O'Meara reports Napoleon to have said to him afterwards: "I never saw such a horrid countenance. He sat on a chair opposite to my sofa, and on the table between us there was a cup of coffee. His physiognomy made such an unfavourable impression upon me, that I thought his looks had poisoned it, and I ordered Marchand to throw it out of window; I could not have swallowed it for the world."

Speaking of a stormy interview with Sir Hudson Lowe, Napoleon said: "I behaved very ill to him, no doubt, and nothing but my present situation could have excused me. I was out of humour; I should blush for it in any other situation. Had such a scene taken place at the Tuileries, I should have felt myself bound in conscience to make some atonement. Never during the period of my power did I speak harshly to any one, without afterwards saying something to make amends for it. Here I uttered not a word of conciliation, and I had no wish to. The Governor proved very insensible to my severity; his delicacy did not seem wounded by it. I should have liked, for his sake, to have seen him evince a little anger, or pull the door violently after him when he went away. This would, at least, have shown that there was some spring and elasticity about him; but I found nothing of the kind."* (May, 1816.)

---

* Napoleon, as Sir Hudson Lowe told him in the conversation referred to, does indeed appear to have totally misunderstood the English character, and to have ignorantly confounded self-control with want of feeling.

In a letter to Sir Thos. Reade (July, 1816,) O'Meara gives part of a conversation Bonaparte held with him. "He asked," says O'Meara, "'What are those *coglioni*, the Commissioners, doing in the town?'

"He asked about Madame Stürmer. I said that she was, I believed, the handsomest, or *one* of the handsomest women in the island.

"'What,' said he, 'is she handsomer than Lady Lowe?'

"He asked about Montchenu, and repeated: 'Poor fool! poor old fool! poor fool!'—(*Povero coglione, povero vecchio coglione*),—several times, with an air of contempt. 'And that coglionaccio, his aide-de-camp, what does he do?'

"I said, I believed he walked up and down the streets with his master.

"'Ah! poor fool,' said he, laughing; and afterwards, 'Poor, imbecile lacquey!' (*Ah! povero miuchione Ragazzachio, povero imbecile!*")

On the 18th of August, Sir Hudson Lowe had his last stormy and unsatisfactory interview with Napoleon. Speaking of it to Las Cases, he said: "I must receive this officer no more, he puts me in a passion; it is beneath my dignity. It would have been more worthy of me, finer and greater, to have expressed all these things with composure; they would, besides, have been more impressive."

On the 16th of October, Bonaparte wrote to Sir Hudson Lowe, requesting permission to take another name. "I am quite ready," said he, "to take any ordinary name; and I repeat, that when it may be deemed proper to release me from this cruel abode, I am resolved to remain a stranger to politics, whatever may be passing in the world. Such is my resolve, and anything which may have been said different from this would not be the fact."

Sir Hudson Lowe, in a letter to Lord Bathurst, relates the following anecdote:—

"Cipriani came out one day from General Bonaparte's room to Dr. O'Meara, saying, in a manner indicating great surprise, 'My master is certainly beginning to lose his head. He begins to believe in God, one would think. He said to the servant, who was shutting the windows: "Why do you take from us the light which God gives us?" Oh, certainly he is losing his head. He began at Waterloo, but it is certain now.'"

The following statement, made by Napoleon to O'Meara, concerning the battle of Waterloo, will be found very interesting, although, undoubtedly, feelings of jealousy towards Wellington and his troops have helped to form his opinions.

"The worst thing that ever England did was endeavouring to make herself a great military nation. In doing so, she must always be the slave of Russia, Prussia, or Austria, or at least in some degree subservient to them, because she has not enough men to combat with France or any other continental nation, and consequently must hire men from some of them; whereas at sea she is so superior, her sailors so much better, that she would always be superior, and could command all the others with safety to herself and but comparatively little expense. Your English soldiers, too, have not the qualities for a military nation; they are not equal in agility, address, or intelligence, to the French, and when they meet with a reverse their discipline is very bad. When they get from under the fear of the lash, you can get them to do nothing, and in a retreat they cannot be managed; and if they meet with wine or spirits they are so many devils, and there is no longer any subordination. I saw myself the retreat of Moore, and I never in my life witnessed anything so bad as the conduct of the soldiers; it was impossible to collect them or make them do anything; nearly all were drunk. The officers, too, depend too much upon interest for promotion. Your army," he continued, " is certainly brave, nobody can deny it. If you had lost the battle of Waterloo what a state England would have been in,—the flower of your army destroyed; for not a man would have escaped, not even Lord Wellington himself."

"I told him here," says O'Meara, "that Lord Wellington had determined never to quit the field of battle *alive.*

" He replied, 'He could not leave it,—he could not retreat; he would have been destroyed with his whole army. He said so himself to that cavalry officer who was wounded. If Grouchy had come up at that time instead of the Prussians, not a man would have escaped.'"

O'Meara asked him if he had not believed for a long time that the Prussians who advanced on his right were Grouchy's division. He replied:

"To be sure I did; and I can even now scarcely account for the reason why it was not Grouchy's division, instead of them."

O'Meara then asked him what he supposed would have been the event if *neither Grouchy* nor the Prussians had come up that day,—if it would not have been a drawn battle,—whether both armies would not have kept their ground?

"No," was his reply, "the English army would have been destroyed; it was defeated before mid-day (*mezzo giorno*). I should have gained everything. I had gained everything. I beat the Prussians; but accident, or more likely *destiny* decided that Lord Wellington should gain it, and he did so. He was fortunate, accident and destiny favoured him. I could scarcely have believed he would have given me battle, because, if he had retreated, as he ought to have done, to Antwerp, I must have been overwhelmed by armies of three or four hundred thousand men coming against me, whom I could not possibly have resisted. Besides, if they intended to give battle, it was the greatest *coglioneria* in the world to separate the Prussian and English armies; they ought to have been united, and I cannot conceive the reason of their separation. It was also *coglioneria* in him to hazard a battle in a place where, if defeated, all must have been lost, for he could not retreat. He would have been altogether destroyed; he suffered himself to be surprised by me. He ought to have had all his army encamped from the beginning of June, as he must have known that I intended to attack him; he might have lost everything by it; it was a great fault on his part; but he has been fortunate, and everything he did will meet with applause. My intentions were to destroy the English army; this I knew would produce an immediate change of ministry. The indignation against the ministry for having caused the loss of forty thousand of the flower of the English army, of the sons of the first families, and others who would have perished there, would have excited such a popular commotion that they would have been turned out; the people would have said, What is it to us who is on the throne of France, Louis or Napoleon? Are we to sacrifice all our blood to place on the throne a detested family? No, we have suffered enough, let them fight it out amongst them; it's no affair of ours! The English would have made peace and withdrawn from the coalition; the Saxons, Bavarians, Belgians, Würtemburgers and others, would have joined me; the Russians would have made peace. I would have been quietly seated on the throne; I would have made peace with all, which would have been permanent, for what could France do after the treaty of Paris? What was to be feared from her? This was my reason for attacking the English. Before twelve o'clock I had succeeded; everything was mine, I might almost say; but destiny and accident decided it otherwise. The English fought bravely, doubtless, but they would have been all destroyed. What would have been the state of the English army after the loss of forty thousand of their best troops? for I suppose there were about so many English in the field."

O'Meara asked if the retaining of Malta by the English was the real cause of the war? At first Napoleon replied that it was, but afterwards seemed to say that the war would have broken out even if that pretext had not been in the way. He added, "Two days before the departure of Lord Whitworth from Paris, he offered to the ministers and others about me *thirty millions* of francs if I would consent that Malta should belong to the English, and also to acknowledge me King of France.

"They send me the 'Times,'" said Napoleon, "that infamous paper, the journal of the Bourbons. When I returned from Elba I found amongst the papers of the Bourbons an account of a sum of 6000 francs monthly paid by them to the *editors* of the 'Times,' with a hundred copies of the papers monthly; I also found the *receipt* of the *editors* acknowledging it, signed by them. He also said that he had received offers from the *editors* of London papers, and amongst others the 'Times,' to write for him for payment even before he went to Elba. He added, 'I am sorry I did not accept their offers, as my name would not have been so hated by the English if I had done so; the papers in England form the public opinion."*

On the 11th of December Napoleon wrote to Las Cases as follows: †

"MY DEAR COUNT DE LAS CASES,— My heart is deeply affected by what you now experience. Torn from me a fortnight ago, you have been ever since closely confined, without the possibility of my receiving any news from you or sending you any; without having had any communication with any person, either French or English; deprived even of the attendance of a servant of your own choice. Your conduct at St. Helena has been like the whole of your life, honourable and irreproachable; I have pleasure in giving you this testimony; your letter to a friend in London contains nothing objectionable; you merely unburden your heart in the bosom of friendship. This letter is similar to eight or ten others which you have written to the same person, and which you have sent unsealed. The governor having had the indelicacy to pry into the expressions

---

* Letter of O'Meara to Mr. Finlaison, dated the 10th of October.

† This was after Las Cases' arrest for endeavouring to send communications, written on silk taffetas, by means of a former mulatto servant of his, to Lady Clavering and Lucien Bonaparte.

which you confide to friendship, has latterly reproached you with them, threatening to send you out of the island if your letters continued to be the bearers of complaints against him. He has thus violated the first duty of his situation, the first article of his instructions, the first sentiment of honour; he has thus authorized you to seek for means to open your heart to your friends, and inform them of the guilty conduct of this governor. But you have been very simple; your confidence has been easily beguiled! A pretext has been wanting to seize upon your papers, but your letter to your friend in London could not authorize a visit from the police to you since it contained neither plot nor mystery; since it was only the expression of a noble and sincere heart. The illegal and precipitate conduct observed on this occasion bears the stamp of a base feeling of personal animosity. In the least civilized countries, exiles, prisoners, and criminals even are under the protection of the laws and magistrates; those persons who are entrusted with the keeping of them have superior officers in the administration who watch over them. On this rock, the man who makes the most absurd regulations, executes them with violence and transgresses all laws; there is no one to check the outrages of his passions. The Prince Regent can never be informed of the acts carried on under his name; they have refused to forward my letters to him; they have in a violent manner sent back the complaints made by Count Montholon; and Count Bertrand has since been informed that no letters would be received if they continued to be libellous as they had hitherto been. Longwood is surrounded by a mystery, which it is sought to render impenetrable in order to conceal a guilty line of conduct which is calculated to create a suspicion of the most criminal intentions!!! By reports insidiously circulated, it is endeavoured to deceive the officers, the travellers, the inhabitants of this island, and even the agents, which, it is said, Austria and Russia have sent here. No doubt the English government is deceived, in like manner, by artful and false representations. They have seized your papers, amongst which they know there were some belonging to me, without the least formality, in the room next to mine, with a ferocious *éclat* and manifestation of joy. I was informed of it afterwards, and looked from the window, when I saw that they were hurrying you away. A numerous staff was prancing round the house; methought I saw the inhabitants of the Pacific ocean dancing round the prisoner they were about to devour. Your company was necessary to me. You are the only one that can read, speak, and understand English. How many nights you have watched over me during my illnesses. However, I advise you, and if necessary, I order you to demand of the governor of this country to send you to the continent;[*] he cannot refuse, since he has no power over you, but by virtue of the act which you have voluntarily signed. It will be a great source of consolation to me to know that you are on your way to more favoured climes. Once in Europe, whether you proceed to England or return home, endeavour to forget the evils which you have been made to suffer; and boast of the fidelity which you have shown towards me, and of all the affection I feel for you. If you should some day or other see my wife and son, embrace them for me; for the

---

[*] O'Meara, in his letter to Mr. Finlaison, of the 29th of December, 1816, says that Napoleon wrote this not knowing that Las Cases would be allowed to return to Longwood, and thinking he would be kept *au secret*.

last two years I have had no news from them either directly or indirectly. There is in this country a German botanist, who has been here for the last six months, and who saw them in the gardens of Schœnbrun a few months before his departure. The barbarians have carefully prevented him from coming to give me any news respecting them. In the meantime, be comforted and console my friends. My body, it is true, is exposed to the hatred of my enemies; they omit nothing that can contribute to satisfy their vengeance; they make me suffer the protracted tortures of a slow death, but Providence is too just to allow these sufferings to last much longer. The insalubrity of this dreadful climate, the want of everything that tends to support life, will soon, I feel, put an end to my existence, the last moments of which will be an opprobrium to the British name; and Europe will one day stigmatize with horror that perfidious and wicked man; all true Englishmen will disown him as a Briton. As there is every reason to suppose that you will not be allowed to come and see me before your departure, receive my embrace and the assurance of my friendship. Yours,

"NAPOLEON." *

"Man is only a more perfect animal than the rest.

---

* A great many of the statements contained in this letter were evidently put forth as a mere ruse to frighten the governor and procure Las Cases' liberation. When Las Cases', on the 5th of December, sent a secret message to Longwood to the effect that he was admirably treated, Napoleon said, "Ha, ha! I am gaining ground. Sir Hudson Lowe is evidently afraid." Again, on the 12th, after dictating to Marchand, a "fine" letter for Las Cases, he sent Gourgaud to fetch it and read it, observing that it "would terribly embarrass the governor."

He reasons better. But who knows that lower animals have not a particular language? I think it is presumption on our part to deny it because we do not know. A horse has memory, knowledge, and sensibility. He distinguishes his master from the servants, although they are more constantly with him. I myself had a horse who distinguished me from all others, and who showed by his curvetings and superb pace, when I was on his back, that he carried a personage superior to those by whom he was surrounded. He only allowed myself and a groom to mount him, and when this man mounted him, his action was so different one would have thought he knew he had only a groom on his back. When I lost my way I threw the reins on his neck, and he always found it. Who can deny the intelligence of dogs? There is a link between all animals. Plants are eating and drinking animals, and there are different gradations up to man, who is the most perfect of all. The same spirit animates them all, more or less." *Napoleon dans l'exil. O'Meara.*

Of his two would-be assassins, Cérachi and the fanatic of Schœnbrun, Napoleon said, "Cérachi adored the consul once, till he said he could see nothing in him but the tyrant. He was assisted by a captain of the line, sought admission for the purpose of altering a bust of me, and intended to stab me when I was posed. This officer of the line disliked me as consul, but adored me as general. He wished my post to be taken from me, but he would have grieved sincerely if they had taken my life. 'They must seize me,' said he, 'not do me any harm, and send me to the army to go on beating the enemy, and to make the glory of France.'" When he saw the poniards distributed he was afraid, and revealed the whole to the consul.

"The fanatic of Schœnbrun," said the Emperor, "was the son of a Protestant minister of Erfurt. He was trying to force his way through the soldiers that surrounded me (it was at grand parade), when General Rapp, placing his hand on his chest to put him back, felt something underneath his coat. It was a two-edged knife, a foot and a half long."

Napoleon had the assassin brought to his cabinet; called Corvisart, and told him to feel the man's pulse whilst he talked to him. The assassin preserved his composure, openly avowed his intention, and frequently quoted Scripture.

"What did you want with me?" said the Emperor.

"To kill you."

"What have I done to you? Who has made you my judge?"

"I wished to put an end to the war."

"And why did you not address yourself to the Emperor Francis?"

"What good would that be? he is nobody! And then when he dies another will succeed him; whereas, after you the French would immediately disappear from Germany."

The Emperor sought in vain to move him.

"Do you repent?" he asked him.

"No."

"Would you do it again?"

"Yes."

"But if I pardoned you?"

"Here," says Napoleon, "nature for an instant resumed her sway, the face and voice of the man altered."

H

"Then," said he, "I should believe that it was not God's will."

"But he soon recovered his ferocity," continues Napoleon. "We made him fast for twenty-four hours; the doctor examined him again; we questioned him anew. All was useless; he remained the same man, or rather ferocious beast, and we left him to his fate."

1817. When Sir Hudson Lowe sent to say that he would enter Napoleon's room, to assure himself that he had not escaped, he sent this message back:—"Tell my jailer that it only remains for him to exchange his keys for the axe of the executioner; and if he enters, it shall be over a corpse. Give me my pistols."

Sir Thomas Strange, one of the first judges in Calcutta, stopping at St. Helena on his way to England, asked through Sir Hudson Lowe, for permission to pay his respects to the emperor. "Tell the governor," said Napoleon to the grand marshal, "that men who have gone down into the tomb do not receive visits; and take care that this Indian judge knows my answer."

"My mother," said Napoleon, "is a woman of much order and great virtue. But like all mothers, she loved her children unequally. Pauline and I were her favourites; Pauline, because she was the prettiest and most graceful; I, perhaps through one of those natural instincts, which told her that I should be the creator of the nobility of her blood. When she came to see me at Brienne, she was so frightened at my thinness and the alteration in my features, that she fancied they had changed me, and hesitated some seconds before recognising me. I was indeed much changed, because I employed the hours of recreation in working, and often passed the nights in meditating upon the day's lessons. My nature could not bear the idea of not being at once the first in my class."

"During my reign, I was wrong for not conversing more frequently with the ladies. I ought to have seen them every day; they have an independence of spirit not found amongst men. How much might I not have learnt from women like Madame de Montmorency. I should then perhaps have got rid of Talleyrand. Madame Bassano, when I took away foreign affairs from her husband, sought me and reproached me for my ingratitude; and spoke to me in a way that I did not understand. I don't know whence she got all she said to me. Madame de Rovigo also attacked me about her husband; she absolutely wanted me to make him a marshal; and recalled his devotion and services to me with unparalleled energy; she almost upset me when she made the mistake of saying to me, 'It is like Sebastiani, whom you neglect, and make your enemy.' 'Ah madame, it is too much,' I exclaimed, 'to plead the cause of your husband at the same time that you speak for your lover.' Not in the least disconcerted, she replied, 'I am no longer young enough to have a lover, you know very well . . . but, I repeat, you ought to manage Sebastiani. He is a man of much intelligence, of great influence in the Parliament, and you ought to make him marshal of France in your own interest. As to Savary, he is different; he will serve you the same whether you are ungrateful to him or not.' Well," continued the Emperor, "she was right; if I had given the marshal's baton to Sebastiani, I should probably have kept the majority in the chamber of deputies; and as he had commanded a corps with distinction, this nomination would not have appeared at all extraordinary to the army."

Napoleon related an anecdote of Général Dejean and his son, who married two sisters. "Is what you have done quite orthodox?" asked Napoleon of the general; "a father and son to marry two sisters?"

"But," the general replied, "your majesty has done worse!"

"How so?"

"You married the mother, and your brother married her daughter."

"I?"

"Certainly; you the Empress Josephine, and your brother Louis the Princess Hortense her daughter."

"My faith, I never thought of that," was the emperor's reply; and, he added at St. Helena smiling, "I told him the truth. I had so many other more important things in my head."

"The contagion of crime is like that of the plague," said Napoleon. "Criminals collected together corrupt each other; they are worse than ever, when at the termination of their punishment they re-enter society."

"At what time of my life do you think I was happiest?" Napoleon asked the grand marshal.

"Undoubtedly, sire, at the birth of the king of Rome."

"—Yes! I was content!"

"At your majesty's marriage?" said Gourgand.

"Happy! no, I was content."

'Consul?"

"I had no distinction."

"Emperor?" asked Montholon.

"Perhaps; but I am inclined to believe that I was happiest at Tilsit. I had experienced vicissitudes, cares, and reverses. Eylau had reminded me that fortune might abandon me, and I found myself victorious, dictating peace, with Emperors and Kings to form my court. After all, that is not a real enjoyment. Perhaps I was really more happy after my Italian victories, hearing the people raise their voices, only to bless their liberator, and all that at twenty-five years of age! From that time, I saw what I might become. I already saw the world flying beneath me, as if I had been carried through the air."

"The Duke of Wellington," said Napoleon, "has been called a human butcher, he is especially blamed for his assault of Badajos. However, it remains to be calculated whether it is better to attack thus, whether the loss is less from the butchery of a day than by the daily, though comparatively insensible loss, of the ordinary course of a siege; and then the time gained is immense."

After reading Buffon, he said, "They may say what they like, everything is organized matter. The tree is the first link of the chain, man is the last. Men are young, the earth is old. Vegetable and animal chemistry are still in their infancy. Electricity, galvanism, what discoveries in a few years!"

Of the bust of Napoleon's son, which had been sent to St. Helena in the Baring, Napoleon, who by some means had heard of its arrival some days previously

(10 June, 1817), said to O'Meara, "I intended if it had not been sent me, to have made such a complaint as would have caused every Englishman's hair to stand on end with horror. I would have told a tale which would have made the mothers of England execrate him (Sir Hudson Lowe) as a monster in human shape."

On November 23rd (1817), Napoleon wrote on the back of a letter of Sir Hudson Lowe to Count Bertrand (bearing date November 18th, 1817, and repudiating the defamatory statements made against him): "This letter, and those of the 26th of July, and 26th of October last, are full of falsehoods. I have confined myself to my room for eighteen months, in order to secure myself against the insults of this officer. At present my health is impaired; it no longer admits of my reading such disgusting writings; send me no more of them. Whether this officer thinks himself authorized by the verbal and secret instructions of his minister, as he gives out, or he acts on his own impulse, which is probable from the pains he takes to fret himself,* I can only treat him as my assassin. If they had sent here a man of honour I should certainly have had some torments the less, but they would have spared themselves the reproaches of Europe and of history, which the trashy writings of this crafty man cannot deceive."

Speaking of his brother Joseph to O'Meara, Napoleon said, "His virtues and talents were suited to a retired

---

* Napoleon appears to have overlooked the fact that he was the prime mover in all the fretful and unnecessary quarrels that were continually taking place between his household and Sir Hudson Lowe.

life; nature destined him for it. He is too good to be a great man. He has no ambition. He is very like me, physically, but he is better than I am. He is extremely well informed, but his acquirements are not suited to a monarchy. Neither is he capable of commanding an army."

Of Blucher, Napoleon said to O'Meara, "Blucher is a very brave soldier, a good swordsman (un bon sabreur) He is like a bull who shuts his eyes and rushes forward, and sees no danger. He committed millions of faults, and *if fortune had not favoured him* I should have taken him prisoner several times, as well as the greater part of his army. He is opinionated, indefatigable, fears nothing, and is attached to his country; but as a general he is without talent. I remember that when I was in Prussia he dined at my table, and was then looked upon as a very ordinary man."

Of the English soldiers, he said on the same occasion, "The English soldier is brave, none more so, and the officers are in general men of honour; but, I do not think them capable of performing great feats. I think that if I were at their head I could make them capable of anything. However, I do not know enough of them yet to form a decided opinion. . . . In place of the lash I would discipline them by honour. I would excite a spirit of emulation in them, and promote them according to their deserts. What might not be hoped from the English army, if each who behaved well had the chance of becoming a general some day!"

"Who eat the most?" Napoleon asked, "the French or the English?"

"The French, I think," O'Meara replied.

"I don't think so," said Napoleon.

O'Meara answered that it was true that the French only took nominally two meals a-day, but that in reality they had four.

"They take only two," he replied.

"They take something at nine o'clock, at eleven, at four, and again at seven or eight in the evening," said O'Meara.

"I never eat more than twice a-day," Napoleon answered, "but you English always four times a-day. Your cuisine is more wholesome than ours, but your soup is very bad; nothing but bread and pepper and water. You drink an enormous quantity of wine."

"Not as much as the French think," was O'Meara's answer.

"Bah!" Napoleon replied. "Piontkowski, who sometimes dines in the camp with the officers of the 53rd says, that they drink by the hour; that after the cloth is removed they pay so much an hour and drink as much as they like, not leaving off sometimes until four in the morning."

"That is so far from being the truth," O'Meara replied, "that there are officers who do not drink wine more than twice a week, and only on the days when strangers may be invited."

"He appeared surprised at this," continues O'Meara, "and observed how easily a stranger who had only an imperfect acquaintance with a language, might misjudge the manners and customs of other nations."

"A humorous conversation," says O'Meara, "took place between us on patron saints. Napoleon asked me who was my patron saint? and after my reply he said:

"Saint Napoleon ought to be much obliged to me, and place all his credit in the other world to my account. The poor devil! no one knew him once, he had not even a day in the calendar. I procured him one, and persuaded the pope to assign to him the 15th of August, my birthday. I remember in Italy," he continued, " hearing a priest preach on the subject of a poor sinner who had quitted this life. He related that his soul appeared before God and that he was obliged to give an account of his actions. The good and evil were then cast into the opposite scales of the balance, to see which of the two was the heavier. The scale containing the good was much lighter, and sprang up immediately. The soul of the sinner was then condemned to the infernal regions, conducted by angels to the bottomless pit, and put into the hands of the devils, who precipitated it into the flames. 'Already,' said the priest, ' the devouring element had seized his legs and feet; it reached his chest; the source of life was gained, oh! my brothers. His head alone at last was above the fiery waves, when he thought of addressing himself, first to God, then to his patron saint: ' O patron,' said he, ' look down upon me; oh! have pity on my poor soul. Cast into the scale with my good actions all the stones that I gave to repair the convent of ———.' His saint immediately heard his prayer. He collected all the stones, and threw them into the scale with the good, which immediately outweighed that containing the evil, and the soul of the sinner went at once to Paradise. 'You see, then, my dear brothers,' the priest continued, ' how necessary it is to repair convents; but for the stones which the sinner gave to rebuild the monastery, his soul would still be burning in the fires of hell; and yet you are so blinded that you allow the church and convent that your ancestors have built to fall in ruins.' At that time," Napoleon concluded, laughing, "these *canaille* wanted their convent rebuilt, and that was the expedient resorted to to gain money, which poured in upon them from all quarters after that."

"When a man has no confidence in his doctor," said Napoleon to O'Meara, "it is useless his having one. One cannot command confidence. You ought to look upon yourself as belonging to no nation in particular. A doctor and a priest should both consider themselves so, they ought to be free from all political bias. Treat me as if I were an Englishman. Chance has placed you near me, and that is why I place confidence in you. If I had not chosen you, you know I should have had a French doctor, who would have sent in no bulletins without my permission. If you attended Lord Bathurst should you send bulletins of the state of his health to others than those of his own family? I beg you will treat me the same, and set on one side all political considerations as to what I am and what I have been; finally, when I consult you, act as you would act to one of your own countrymen who was ill."

Of Cornwallis, Napoleon said to O'Meara: "Cornwallis was an honest, generous, and sincere man, a very brave man. He was the first who gave me a good opinion of the English; his integrity, his fidelity, his candour, and the nobility of his sentiments, gave me a favourable opinion of you. I remember that Cornwallis said one day, 'There are some qualities that can be acquired, but a good character, sincerity, a noble pride and courage in the midst of danger cannot be acquired.' These words made an impression on me. At

Amiens, I gave him, for amusement, a regiment of cavalry, the officers of which liked him much; I do not think he was a man of the first order of merit, but he had talent, and was very honest and sincere. He never broke his word. At Amiens the treaty was ready, and he was to sign it at nine o'clock at the Hôtel de Ville. Something happened to hinder him from going, but he sent word to the French ministers that they might consider the treaty signed, and that he would sign it the next day. A courier arrived that evening from England bringing him an order to refuse his consent to certain articles of the treaty, and not to sign it. Although Cornwallis had not signed it, and could easily have taken advantage of this order, he had sufficient loyalty to say that he considered his promise equivalent to his signature; he wrote to his Government saying that he had promised, and that having once given his word he should keep it, that if they were not satisfied they could refuse to ratify the treaty. There is a man of honour, a true Englishman. It is a man like Cornwallis that they ought to have sent here as a governor, instead of such a composition of lying, suspicion, and baseness. I was very grieved when I heard of his death. Some members of his family wrote to me occasionally in favour of certain prisoners. I always granted what they wished."

1818. "It has been said," said Napoleon, "that the marriage of Marie Louise was one of the secret articles of the treaty of Vienna, which had been concluded some months before; that is entirely false. An alliance with Austria had never been dreamed of before the despatch of Narbonne, which mentioned the overtures that the emperor Francis and Metternich had made to him. Indeed this marriage with the Empress Marie Louise was proposed in the council, discussed, decided, and signed within twenty-four hours; which fact can be attested by a great number of the council still alive. Many were of opinion that I should have married a Frenchwoman; and the arguments in favour of this proposition were so strong that I hesitated a moment. However, the court of Austria insinuated that if I refused to choose a princess from one of the reigning Houses of England, it would be a tacit declaration that I intended to overthrow them when an opportunity presented itself."

Speaking of men, Napoleon said, " You do not know men; they are difficult to understand when one wishes to be just; do they know themselves? do they explain themselves? The greater number of those who abandoned me, had I continued to be fortunate, would not have thought themselves capable of such conduct. There are the vices and virtues of circumstances; our last experiences are above all human power; and then I have been abandoned rather than betrayed. There has been more weakness about me than treachery; it is the denial of St. Peter, *repentance and tears may be at the gate.* Besides that, who in all history had more partizans and friends? Who was more popular and more beloved? Who ever left sharper and more ardent regrets? Kings and princes, my allies, have been faithful unto death. They have been taken away by the people in a mass; and those of my own who were around me were enveloped and deprived of their senses in an irresistible whirlwind. No; human nature could show itself more hideous, and I might have more to complain of."

"I have often asked myself the question whether I did for my unhappy people all that they had a right to expect; they did so much for me. History shall decide. What is very certain is, that I am far from shunning its verdict; I court it. Will that people ever know all that the night preceding my final decision cost me, that night of uncertainty and anguish? Two ways were left to me. I did right to take the one I did, *friends and enemies, well intentioned and ill intentioned, all were against me.* I was alone. It was time to give up. I did so, and once done it was done for ever; I am not for half measures. The other way called for a strange vigour. There were great criminals, and heavy punishments would have been necessary. Blood might flow, and then who knows whither we should have been led? and what scenes might have been renewed? But if at this price I had saved the country, I was full of energy, but was I certain of success? Which of the crowd of fools surrounding me could I have persuaded that I was not working for myself, for my personal advantage? which of them should I have convinced that I was disinterested; that I only fought to save the country? Which of them would have believed all the dangers, all the misfortunes from which I sought to free them? I could see them, but as to the common herd they never saw them unless they weighed heavily on each. What might they have replied to that which was cried: Here he is again, the despot, the tyrant! The day after his oaths are made, he breaks them again! And who knows if in all these movements, this inextricable complication, I might not have perished by a French hand in this citizen conflict. And then what would have become of the nation in the eyes of all the world, and in the esteem of the remotest generations? for her glory is to own me. I should not know how to have done so many things for her honour, her glory, without her, in spite of her. She would make me too great! ... I repeat it, history will decide."

"Bernadotte," said Napoleon, "showed himself ungrateful to me, who was the author of his elevation, but I cannot say that he betrayed me. He became Swedish in some manner, and never promised what he did not intend to perform. I can accuse him of ingratitude but not of treason. Neither Murat nor he would have declared against me had they known it would have cost me my throne. They desired to weaken my power, not to overthrow me entirely. The bravery of Murat was so great that the Cossacks were accustomed to relieve the feelings it produced in them, by cries of admiration. They could not help experiencing a sentiment of respect on seeing this man of a noble and imposing figure, advancing like an old knight, and performing similar prodigies of valour. Labédoyère was a young man animated with the noblest sentiments. He had the most sovereign contempt for a race surrounded by all that was most foreign to the manners and rights of the French, a race given up to a set of *misérables*, who, not to die of hunger, had vegetated for twenty-five years in low and degrading conditions. His attachment to me was quite enthusiastic, and he declared himself in my favour at the moment of the greatest danger."

Napoleon said to O'Meara when the latter was leaving St. Helena, "When you arrive in Europe, you will go yourself, or send some one to my brother Joseph. You will let him know that I wish him to give you the packet containing the private and confidential letters,* that the emperors Alexander and Francis, the king of Prussia, and the other sovereigns of Europe addressed to me, and which I gave to him at Rochfort. You will publish them to *cover with shame* those sovereigns, and to let the world see, the abject homage these vassals paid me when they asked favours, or begged me to leave them their thrones. When I was powerful and strong, they *craved my protection and the honour of my alliance;* they licked the dust under my feet. Now, they oppress me in my old age, they take away my wife and child. I beg you to do this for me, and if you hear any public calumnies against me while you have been here with me, and you can say, 'I know of my own knowledge that that is not true,' contradict them."

1819. The following trifling circumstance will serve to show how sensitive Napoleon was on the subject of the slightest intrusion at Longwood, and how little he was disposed to show any civility to Mr. Baxter. Mr. Baxter having been invited to dine at Longwood on the 8th of December, with Captain Nicholls and Dr. Verling, went there about 6 o'clock in the evening, in company with Major Power. They both went to look at the new building that was going on, and saw Napoleon at the window going and returning. A few days after, Count Montholon called on Captain Nicholls with the following message: "Tell the orderly officer that a few days ago I saw Dr. Baxter walking round my house, that I conceive his doing so an indelicate intrusion after

---

* Unfortunately, says O'Meara, all the efforts I made to obtain these important papers, on my return to Europe were unsuccessful.

the communication respecting that person, and the protestations I some time since made against receiving him as my medical attendant; and that I desire that the orderly officer will in future prevent Dr. Baxter from walking about my residence; and further, should Dr. Baxter think fit to make a bulletin of the state of my health in consequence, I protest against such proceedings."

Of the Saviour Napoleon said, in conversation with General Bertrand, "I know men, and I tell you that Jesus Christ is not a man. Superficial minds see a resemblance between Christ and the founders of empires, and the gods of other religions. That resemblance does not exist. There is between Christianity and all other religions whatsoever, the distance of infinity.

"To the authors of every other religion we can say, You are neither gods nor the agents of deity. You are but missionaries of falsehood, moulded from the same clay with the rest of mortals. You are made with all the passions and vices inseparable from them. Your temples and your priests proclaim your origin. Such will be the judgment, the cry of conscience of whoever examines the gods and the temples of paganism.

"Paganism was never accepted as truth by the wise men of Greece, neither by Socrates, Pythagoras, Plato, Anaxagoras, nor Pericles. But, on the other side, the loftiest intellects, since the advent of Christianity have had faith, a living faith, a practical faith, in the mysteries and doctrines of the gospel; not only Bossuet and Fénelon, who were preachers, but Descartes and Newton, Leibnitz and Pascal, Corneille and Racine, Charlemagne and Louis XIV. Paganism is the work of man. One can here read but our imbecility. What do these gods, so boastful, know more than other mortals? these legislators, Greek or Roman? this Numa, this Lycurgus? these priests of India or of Memphis? this Confucius, this Mohammed? Absolutely nothing. They have made a perfect chaos of morals. There is not one among them all who has said anything new in reference to our future destiny, to the soul, to the essence of God, to the creation. Enter the sanctuaries of Paganism—you there find perfect chaos, a thousand contradictions, war between the gods, the immobility of sculpture, the division and the rending of unity, the parceling out of the divine attributes, mutilated or denied in their essence, the sophisms of ignorance and presumption, polluted fêtes, impurity and abomination adored, all sorts of corruption festering in the thick shades, with the rotten wood, the idol, and his priest. Does this honour God, or does it dishonour him? Are these religions and these gods to be compared with Christianity? As for me I say, No. I summon entire Olympus to my tribunal. I judge the gods, but am far from prostrating myself before their vain images. The gods, the legislators of India and of China, of Rome and of Athens, have nothing which can overawe me. Not that I am unjust to them; no, I appreciate them, because I know their value. Undeniably, princes whose existence is fixed in the memory as an image of order and of power, as the ideal of force and beauty, such princes were no ordinary men.

"I see in Lycurgus, Numa, and Mohammed only legislators, who, having the first rank in the state, have sought the best solution of the social problem; but I see nothing there which reveals divinity. They themselves have never raised their pretensions so high. As for me, I recognize the gods and these great men as beings like myself. They have performed a lofty part in their times, as I have done. Nothing announces them divine. On the contrary, there are numerous resemblances between them and myself, foibles and errors which ally them to me and to humanity.

"It is not so with Christ. Everything in Him astonishes me. His spirit overawes me, and his will confounds me. Between Him and whoever else in the world there is no possible term of comparison. He is truly a being by himself, his ideas and his sentiments, the truths which He announces, his manner of convincing, are not explained either by human organization or by the nature of things.

"His birth, and the history of his life; the profundity of his doctrine, which grapples the mightiest difficulties, and which is of those difficulties the most admirable solution; his gospel, his apparition, his empire, his march across the ages and the realms, everything is to me a prodigy, an insoluble mystery, which plunges me into a reverie from which I cannot escape, a mystery which is there before my eyes, a mystery which I can neither deny nor explain. Here I see nothing human.

"The nearer I approach, the more carefully I examine; everything is above me, everything remains grand—of a grandeur which overpowers. His religion is a revelation from an intelligence which certainly is not that of man. In it is a profound originality which has created a series of words and maxims before unknown. Jesus borrowed nothing from our sciences. One can absolutely find nowhere, but in him alone, the imitation or the example of his life. He is not a philosopher, since he advances by miracles, and from the first his disciples worshipped him. He persuades them far more by an appeal to the heart than by any display of method and of logic. Neither did he impose upon them any preliminary studies, or any knowledge of letters. All his religion consists in *believing*.

" In fact, the sciences and philosophy avail nothing for salvation; and Jesus came into the world to reveal the mysteries of heaven, and the laws of the Spirit. Also, he has nothing to do but with the soul, and to that alone He brings his Gospel. The soul is sufficient for him as he is sufficient for the soul. Before Him the soul was nothing. Matter and time were the masters of the world. At his voice everything returns to order. Science and philosophy become secondary. The soul has reconquered its sovereignty. All the scholastic scaffolding falls, as a ruined edifice, before one single word—*faith*. What a master and what a word which can effect such a revolution! With what authority does he teach men to pray! He imposes his belief, and no one, thus far, has been able to contradict him; first, because the Gospel contains the purest morality, and also because the doctrine which it contains of obscurity, is only the proclamation and the truth of that which exists where no eye can see and no reason can penetrate. Who is the insensate man who will say *no* to the intrepid voyager who recounts the marvels of the icy peaks which he alone has had the boldness to visit? Christ is that bold voyager. One can doubtless remain incredulous, but no one can venture to say *it is not so*.

"Moreover, consult the philosophers upon those mysterious questions which relate to the essence of man and to the essence of religion. What is their response? Where is the man of good sense who has ever learned anything from the system of metaphysics, ancient or modern, which is truly a vain and pompous ideology without any connection with our domestic life, with our passions? Unquestionably, with skill in thinking, one can seize the key of the philosophy of Socrates and Plato; but to do this it is necessary to be a metaphysician; and moreover with years of study one must possess special aptitude. But good sense alone, the heart, an honest spirit, are sufficient to comprehend Christianity.

" The Christian religion is neither ideology nor metaphysics, but a practical rule which directs the actions of man, corrects him, counsels him, and assists him in all his conduct. The Bible contains a complete series of facts, and of historical men to explain time and eternity, such as no other religion has to offer. If this is not the true religion, one is very excusable in being deceived, for everything in it is grand and worthy of God. I search in vain in history to find a parallel to Jesus Christ, or anything which can approach the Gospel. Neither history, nor humanity, nor the ages, nor nature, can offer me anything with which I am able to compare it or explain it. Here everything is extraordinary. The more I consider the Gospel the more I am assured that there is nothing there which is not beyond the march of events, and above the human mind. Even the impious themselves have never dared to deny the sublimity of the Gospel, which inspires them with a sort of compulsory veneration. What happiness that book procures for those who believe it! What marvels those who reflect upon it admire in it! The only book where the mind finds a moral beauty before unknown, and an idea of the Supreme superior even to that which creation suggests! Who but God could produce that type, that ideal of perfection, equally exclusive and original.

" Christ, having but a few weak disciples, was condemned to death. He died the object of the wrath of the Jewish priests and of the contempt of the nation, abandoned and denied by his own disciples.

"'They are about to take me and to crucify me,' said He, 'I shall be abandoned of all the world. My chief disciple will deny me at the commencement of my punishment. I shall be left to the wicked. But then divine justice being satisfied, original sin being expiated by my sufferings, the bond of man to God will be renewed, and my death will be the life of my disciples. Then they will be more strong without me than with me, for they will see me rise again, I shall ascend to the skies, and I shall send to them from heaven a Spirit who will instruct them. The spirit of the cross will enable them to understand my Gospel. In fine, they will believe it, they will preach it, and they will convert the world.'

"And this strange promise so aptly called by Paul the 'foolishness of the cross,' this prediction of one miserably crucified, is literally accomplished, and the mode of the accomplishment is perhaps more prodigious than the promise.

"It is not a day nor a battle which has decided it. Is it the lifetime of a man? No! It is a war, a long combat of three hundred years, commenced by the apostles and continued by their successors and by succeeding generations of Christians. In this conflict all the kings and all the forces of the earth were arrayed on one side. Upon the other I see no army, but a mysterious energy, individuals scattered here and there in all parts of the globe, having no other rallying sign than a common faith in the mysteries of the cross.

"What a mysterious symbol! the instrument of the punishment of the Man-God. His disciples were armed with it. 'The Christ,' they said, 'God has died for the salvation of men.' What a strife, what a tempest these simple words have raised around the humble standard of the sufferings of the Man-God! On the one side we see rage and all the furies of hatred and violence; on the other there is gentleness, moral courage, infinite resignation. For three hundred years spirit struggled against the brutality of sense, the conscience against despotism, the soul against the body, virtue against all the vices. The blood of Christians flowed in torrents. They died kissing the hand which slew them. The soul alone protested while the body surrendered itself to all tortures. Everywhere Christians fell, and everywhere they triumphed.

"You speak of Cæsar, of Alexander, of their conquests, and of the enthusiasm they enkindled in the hearts of their soldiers; but can you conceive of a dead man making conquests with an army faithful and entirely devoted to his memory? My armies have forgotten me, even while living, as the Carthaginian army forgot Hannibal. Such is our power! A single battle lost crushes us, and adversity scatters our friends.

"Can you conceive of Cæsar, the eternal emperor of the Roman senate, from the depths of his mausoleum governing the empire, watching over the destinies of Rome? Such is the history of the invasion and conquest of the world by Christianity. Such is the power of the God of the Christians, and such is the perpetual miracle of the progress of the faith and of the government of his church. Nations pass away, thrones crumble, but the Church remains. What is then the power which has protected this Church thus assailed by the furious billows of rage and the hostility of ages? Where is the arm which, for eighteen hundred years has protected the Church from so many storms which have threatened to engulf it?

"In every other existence but that of Christ how

many imperfections! Where is the character which has not yielded, vanquished by obstacles? Where is the individual who has never been governed by circumstances or places, who has never succumbed to the influence of the times, who has never compounded with any customs or passions? From the first day to the last he is the same, always the same, majestic and simple, infinitely firm and infinitely gentle. Truth should embrace the universe. Such is Christianity, the only religion which destroys sectional prejudice, the only one which proclaims the unity and the absolute brotherhood of the whole human family, the only one which is purely spiritual—in fine, the only one which assigns to all without distinction for a true country the bosom of the creator God. Christ proved that he was the Son of the Eternal by his disregard *of Time*. All his doctrines signify one and the same thing—ETERNITY.

"It is true that Christ proposed to our faith a series of mysteries. He commands with authority that we should believe them, giving no other reason than those tremendous words '*I am God*.' He declares it. What an abyss he creates by that declaration between himself and all the fabricators of religion! What audacity, what sacrilege, what blasphemy if it were not true! I say more, the universal triumph of an affirmation of that kind, if the triumph were not really that of God himself, would be a plausible excuse, and a reason for atheism.

"Moreover, in propounding mysteries Christ is harmonious with nature, which is profoundly mysterious. From whence do I come? whither do I go? who am I? Human life is a mystery in its origin, its organization, and its end. In man and out of man, in nature, everything is mysterious. And can one wish that religion should not be mysterious? The creation and the destiny of the world are an unfathomable abyss, as also is the creation and the destiny of each individual. Christianity, at least, does not evade these great questions. It meets them boldly. And our doctrines are a solution of them for every one who believes.

"The Gospel possesses a secret virtue, a mysterious efficacy, a warmth which penetrates and soothes the heart. One finds in meditating upon it, that which one experiences in contemplating the heavens. The Gospel is not a book; it is a living being, with an action, a power which invades everything that opposes its extension. Behold it upon this table, this Book surpassing all others" (here he solemnly placed his hand upon it); "I never omit to read it, and every day with the same pleasure. Nowhere is to be found such a series of beautiful ideas, admirable moral maxims, which defile like the battalions of a celestial army, and which produce in our soul the same emotion which one experiences, in contemplating the infinite expanse of the skies, resplendent in a summer's night with all the brilliance of the stars. Not only is our mind absorbed, it is controlled, and the soul can never go astray with this book for its guide. Once master of our spirit, the faithful Gospel loves us. God even is our friend, our father, and truly our God. The mother has no greater care for the infant whom she nurses.

"What a proof of the divinity of Christ! With an empire so absolute, he has but one single end, the spiritual amelioration of individuals, the purity of conscience, the union to that which is true, the holiness of the soul.

"Christ speaks, and at once generations become his by stricter, closer ties than those of blood—by the most sacred, the most indissoluble of all ties. He lights up the flame of love which consumes self-love, which prevails over every other love. The founders of other religions never conceived of this mystical love, which is the essence of Christianity, and is beautifully called charity. In every attempt to effect this thing, namely, *to make himself beloved*, man deeply feels his own impotence. So that Christ's greatest miracle undoubtedly is the reign of charity.

"I have so inspired multitudes that they would die for me. God forbid that I should form any comparison between the enthusiasm of the soldier and Christian charity, which are as unlike as their cause. But after all, my presence was necessary; the lightning of my eye, my voice, a word from me, then the sacred fire was kindled in their hearts. I do, indeed, possess the secret of this magical power, which lifts the soul; but I could never impart it to any one. None of my generals ever learned it from me; nor have I the means of perpetuating my name, and love for me, in the hearts of men, and to effect these things without physical means.

"Now that I am at St. Helena,—now that I am alone, chained upon this rock, who fights and wins empires for me? who are the courtiers of my misfortune, who thinks of me? who makes efforts for me in Europe? Where are my friends? Yes, two or three whom your fidelity immortalizes, you share, you console my exile."

Here the voice of the Emperor trembled with emotion, and for a moment he was silent. Then he continued:

"Yes, our life once shone with all the brilliance of the diadem and the throne; and yours, Bertrand, reflected that splendour, as the dome of the Invalides, gilt by us, reflects the rays of the sun. But disasters came;

the gold gradually became dim. The ruin of misfortune and outrage with which I am daily deluged has effaced all the brightness. We are mere lead now, General Bertrand and I shall soon be in the grave.

"Such is the fate of great men! So it was with Cæsar and Alexander. And I too am forgotten. And the name of a conqueror and an emperor is a college theme. Our exploits are tasks given to pupils by their tutor, who sit in judgment upon us, awarding censure or praise. And mark what is soon to become of me! assassinated by the English oligarchy, I die before my time; and my dead body, too, must return to the earth, to become food for worms. Behold the destiny near at hand of him who has been called the great Napoleon! What an abyss between my deep misery and the eternal reign of Christ, which is proclaimed, loved, adored, and which is extending over all the earth. Is this to die? Is it not rather to live? The death of Christ! It is the death of God." Turning to General Bertrand: "If you do not perceive that Jesus Christ is God, very well; then I did wrong to make you a general."

When little Arthur Bertrand was inclined to be bad-tempered, Napoleon said to Dr. Antommarchi: "This little fellow is as independent as I was at his age; but the fits of passion to which I gave way proceeded from more excusable motives: I leave you to judge. I had been placed in a school of young ladies, the mistress of which was known to our family; and being a pretty boy and the only one there, I was caressed by every one of my fair schoolfellows. I might generally be seen with my stockings half over my shoes; and in our walks I constantly held the hand of a charming little girl, who was the cause of many broils and quarrels. My malicious comrades, jealous of my Giacominetta, combined these two circumstances together in a song which they made, and whenever I appeared in the street, they followed me singing:

'Napoleone di mezza calzetta
Fa l'amore a Giacominetta.'*

I could not bear to be laughed at; and seizing sticks or stones, or anything that came in my way, I rushed into the midst of the crowd. Fortunately, it always happened that somebody interfered, and got me out of the scrape; but the number opposed to me never stopped me. I never reckoned how many they were."

Speaking to Antommarchi of the battle of Marengo, and mentioning that the Austrian cavalry was half a league off, and required a quarter of an hour to arrive on the field of action, he said: " I have observed that it is always those quarters of an hour that decide the fate of a battle."

"At the height at which we are (2,000 feet) vegetation and life cease," said Napoleon to the Doctor. "British magnanimity had its motives for hoisting me up here."

"Doctor," said Napoleon, "where is France and its cheerful climate? If I could but see it once more! If I could but breathe a little air that had passed over that happy country! What a specific is the soil that gave us birth! Antæus renewed his strength by touching the earth; and I feel that this prodigy would be repeated in

---

* Napoleon, with stockings half down, makes love to Giacominetta.

me, and that I should revive on perceiving our coasts. Our coasts! Ah! I had forgotten that cowardice has taken victory by surprise; its decisions are without appeal."

"My father," said Napoleon, "who was far from being religiously inclined, and who had even composed some anti-religious poetry, no sooner saw the grave half opened, than he became passionately fond of priests! He wished for them—called for them; there were not priests enough in Montpellier to satisfy him. A change so sudden, which, however, occurs in the case of every individual labouring under a serious illness, can only be accounted for by the disorder into which the disease throws the human frame. The organs become blunted, their reaction ceases, the moral faculties are shaken; the head is gone, and thence the desire for confession, *oremuses*, and all the fine things, without which, it seems, we cannot die. But see man in the plenitude of his powers; see those columns ready to march on the field of battle; the drum beats the charge—they rush forward—the cannon roars—they fall; and priests and confession are out of the question."

"I was called Napoleon," he said, "the name which for centuries past was given to the second sons of our family, in order to perpetuate the remembrance of our connection with a certain *Napoleon des Ursins*, celebrated in the 'Records of Italy,'" (p. 269, vol. i).

"Here," said Napoleon to the Doctor, "place this child (the portrait of his son) by the side of his mother; there nearer to the mantel-piece. That is Maria Louisa. She holds her son in her arms. The two others are portraits of Josephine. I loved her tenderly. The ornaments of my mantel-piece are, as you see, not very sumptuous. The bust of my son, two candlesticks, two gilt cups, two vials of Cologne water, a pair of scissors, and a small glass, are all it contains. This is no longer the splendour of the Tuileries. But no matter. If I am decayed in my power, I am not in my glory. I preserve all my recollections. Few sovereigns have immolated themselves for their people. A sacrifice so immense is not without its charms."

"If St. Helena were France, I should love even this frightful rock."

Napoleon occasionally sent for General Bertrand's children. After they had left he would say:

"How happy they are when I send for them or play with them! All their wishes are satisfied. Passions have not yet approached their hearts. They feel the plenitude of existence. Let them enjoy it. At their age I thought and felt as they do. But what storms since! How much that little Hortensia grows and improves! If she lives, of how many young *élégans* will she not disturb the repose? I shall then be no more."

"We men," said Napoleon, on one occasion, when Madame Bertrand was ill; "we men are accustomed to pains and privations, and can bear them; but a woman deprived all at once of everything that tends to render life cheerful and agreeable, transported to a frightful rock, how much more is she to be pitied, and how much resignation she requires! Madame Bertrand, in consequence of her illness, rises late. She cannot attend mass, and yet she would perhaps be glad to hear it said. I did not reflect that she is an invalid, when I fixed the hour of the service. I only considered the great age of the good old abbé. Tell her that I order Vignali to go and officiate at her house. Let her inform Vignali of the hour that suits her. He may construct a moveable altar or use ours. Any person may go to that mass whom the countess thinks proper to admit."

"Tell me," said Napoleon to Dr. Antommarchi, "you, who have searched the human frame in all its windings, have you ever met with the soul under your scalpel? Where does the soul reside? In what organ? Why is it that physicians do not believe in God? *Mathematicians* are generally religious."

Discussing the dogmas of what is called *Legitimacy*, "What ridiculous pretensions," said Napoleon, "what contradictions! Are these principles of legitimacy in conformity with the Scripture—with the laws and maxims of religion? Are nations simple enough to believe themselves the property of a family? Was David, who dethroned Saul, a legitimate? Had he any other rights than those he derived from the consent of his nation. In France, various families have succeeded each other on the throne, and have formed several dynasties, either by the will of the people, represented in their assemblies, or by the votes of the parliaments composed of barons and bishops, who, at that period, represented the nation. How many families have also successively occupied the throne of England. The house of Hanover, which succeeded the prince it dethroned, now reigns, because such was the will of the ancestors of these *touchy people* who thought this change of government absolutely necessary to the preservation of their interests, and of their political and religious rights. Some of the old men still living have witnessed the efforts made by the last branch of the Stuarts to land in Scotland, where they were seconded by those whose ideas and sentiments were conformable to their own. The attempt was opposed, and the Stuarts expulsed by an immense majority of the people, whose new interests and opinions were opposed to those of that degenerate family."

On the 26th of July, as he was reclining on a sofa, he said to Antommarchi, "You, doctor, are strongly attached to me. You regard not contrarieties, pain, and fatigue when you cannot relieve my sufferings: yet all that is not maternal solicitude. Ah! Mamma Letitia," he exclaimed, burying his face in his hands.

"When I was a child," Napoleon confided to Antommarchi, "I was noisy and quarrelsome, and feared nobody. But the affection of Mamma Letitia was tempered by severity. She punished and rewarded without partiality. Nothing we did, either good or evil, was lost. She watched over her children with unexampled care; discarding and stamping with disgrace every ignoble sentiment and affection, and only allowing our young minds to imbibe impressions of what was great and elevated. She abhorred falsehood, punished disobedience, and did not allow any fault to pass unnoticed."

1820. "When my health is restored," said Napoleon to Antommarchi, "I shall restore you to your studies, you shall proceed to Europe and publish your works. I will not suffer you to waste your existence on this horrible rock. You have told me, if I recollect rightly, that you do not know France. You will then see that country. You will see the canals and monuments with which I covered it during the time of my power. The duration of that power has been like that of a flash of lightning. But no matter, it is filled with useful institutions.

"I have hallowed the revolution by infusing into it our laws. My code is the sheet-anchor which will save France, and entitle me to the benedictions of posterity. The plan of levelling the Alps was one of the first formed at the commencement of my career. I had entered Italy, and finding that the communications with Paris occupied a considerable time, and were attended with much difficulty, I endeavoured to render them quicker, and resolved to open them through the valley of the Rhone. I also wished to render that river navigable, and blow up the rock under which it engulfs and disappears. I sent engineers to the spot. The expense would have been inconsiderable, and I submitted the plan to the Directory. But we were carried away by events. I went to Egypt and no one thought any more about it.

"On my return I took it up again. I had dismissed the lawyers, and having no more obstacles in my way, we applied our hammers to the Alps. We executed what the Romans had not dared to try, and traced through blocks of granite, a solid and spacious road, capable of resisting the efforts of time."

"Doctor, what a delightful thing rest is! The bed has become a place of luxury to me! I would not exchange it for all the thrones in the world. What an alteration! How fallen am I! I, whose activity was boundless, whose mind never slumbered, am now plunged in a lethargic stupor and must make an effort, even to raise my eyelids. I sometimes dictated upon different subjects to four or five secretaries who wrote as fast as words could be uttered; but then I was Napoleon, now I am no longer anything. My strength, my faculties forsake me. I do not live; I merely exist."

"You are aware, Doctor" (to Antommarchi), "that the art of healing consists only in lulling and calming the imagination. That is the reason why the ancients dressed up in robes and adopted a costume striking and imposing. That costume you have unadvisedly abandoned; and in so doing you have exposed the imposture of Galen, and no longer exercise the same powerful influence over your patients. Who knows whether, if you were suddenly to appear before me with an enormous wig, a cap, and a long train, I should not take you for the god of health! whereas you are only the god of medicines."*

1821. On the 16th of April Napoleon wrote a codicil to his will as follows: "1st. I desire that my ashes shall repose on the banks of the Seine, in the midst of the French people whom I loved so much.

"2nd. I bequeath to Counts Bertrand and Montholon, and to Marchand, the money, jewels, silver, china, furniture, books, arms, and all that belongs to me at St. Helena. This codicil written entirely by my hand, is signed and sealed with my arms.

" (Seal) NAPOLEON."

"The priests were the class of men that gave me the least trouble," Napoleon said. "They were at first all against me; I allowed them to wear violet-coloured stockings, and from that moment they were all for me."

"Ferdinand of Spain," said the Emperor, "is a man incapable of governing himself, and of course he is

---

* See note.

incapable of governing the Peninsula.* As for the revolution in Naples, I must confess that I did not expect it. Who would ever have supposed that a set of Maccheronai would ape the Spaniards, proclaim their principles, and rival them in courage? No doubt that, of the two Ferdinands, one is not better than the other. But the question does not turn upon them, it is upon their respective nations, and between these there is so great a difference in point of energy and elevation of sentiment, that either the Neapolitans are mad, or this movement of theirs is the forerunner of a general insurrection. In the presence, as they are, of the rulers of Italy, what can they do if they are not supported by some great nation? If they are thus supported, I applaud their patriotism; but if it be otherwise, how much I pity my good and dear Italians! They will be immolated, and the sacrifice of their generous blood will not benefit the beautiful soil which gave them birth. I pity them. Unfortunate people! they are distributed in groups, divided, separated among a parcel of princes who only serve to excite aversions, to dissolve the ties which unite them, and to prevent them from agreeing together and co-operating with each other for the attainment of their common liberty. It was that *tribelike* spirit I was endeavouring to destroy. It was with a view to gain this object that I annexed part of Italy to France, and formed a kingdom of the other part. I wanted to eradicate local habits, partial and narrow views, to model the inhabitants after our manners, to accustom them to our laws, and then to unite them together, and restore them to the ancient glory of Italy.

---

* On the arrival at St. Helena of the intelligence of the revolutionary movements in Spain and Naples.

"I proposed to make of all these states thus agglomerated a compact and independent power, over which my second son would have reigned, and of which Rome restored and embellished would have been the capital. I should have removed Murat from Naples. From the sea to the Alps only one sway would have been acknowledged. I had already commenced the execution of that plan which I had formed with a view to the interest of Italy. Workmen were already engaged in clearing Rome of its ruins, and in draining the Pontine Marshes. But war, the circumstances in which I was placed, and the sacrifices I was obliged to ask of the people, did not allow me to do for them what I wished. Such, my dear doctor, were the motives which stopped me.

"Ah! doctor, what recollections, what epochs, that beautiful Italy recalls to my mind. Methinks the moment is only just gone by when I took the command of the army which conquered it. I was young, like you. I possessed your vivacity, your ardour. I felt the consciousness of my powers, and burned to enter the lists. I had already given proof of what I could do. My aptitude was not contested, but my youth displeased those old soldiers who had grown gray on the field of battle. Perceiving this I felt the necessity of compensating the disadvantage by an austerity of principles from which I never departed. Brilliant actions were required to conciliate the confidence and affection of the military, and I performed some. We marched, and everything vanished at our approach. My name was soon as dear to the people as to the soldiers. I could not be insensible to this unanimity of homage, and became indifferent to everything short of glory. The air resounded with acclamations on my passage. Everything was at my disposal. But I only thought of my brave soldiers, of France, and of posterity."

"Music," said Napoleon, "of all the liberal arts has the greatest influence over the passions, and is that to which the legislator ought to give the greatest encouragement. A well-composed song strikes the mind and softens the feelings, and produces a greater effect than a moral work, which convinces our reason, but does not warm our feelings, nor effect the slightest alteration in our habits."

"It is almost beyond my power to take medicines," said Napoleon. "The aversion I feel for them is almost inconceivable. I exposed myself to dangers with indifference. I saw death without emotion; but I cannot, notwithstanding all my efforts, approach my lips to a cup containing the slightest preparation. True it is that I am a spoiled child, who has never had anything to do with physic." Then turning to Madame Bertrand, who was very ill, he said, "How do you manage to take all those pills and drugs which the doctor is constantly prescribing for you?"

"I take them," she answered, "without thinking about it, and I advise your majesty to do the same."

He shook his head, and asked General Montholon the same question, receiving a similar answer.

"I am then," he said, "the only one who rebels against medicine. I will do so no longer. Give me the stuff." He seized the cup, as if afraid that his determination would fail, and swallowed the dose.

To Count Montholon Napoleon dictated the following counsel for his son:—

"My son should not think of avenging my death. He should profit by it. Let the remembrance of what I have done never leave his mind. Let him always be like me, every inch a Frenchman. The aim of all his efforts should be to reign by peace. If he should recommence my wars out of pure love of imitation, and without any absolute necessity, he would be a mere ape. To do my work over again would be to suppose that I had done nothing. To complete it, on the contrary, would be to show the solidity of the basis, and explain the whole plan of an edifice which I had only roughly sketched. The same thing is not done twice in a century. I was obliged to daunt Europe by my arms. In the present day the way is to convince her. I saved the revolution which was about to perish. I raised it from its ruins and showed it to the world beaming with glory. I have implanted new ideas in France and in Europe. They cannot retrograde. Let my son bring into blossom all that I have sown. Let him develop all the elements of prosperity enclosed in the soil of France, and by these means he may yet be a great sovereign.

"The Bourbons will not maintain their position after my death. A reaction in my favour will take place everywhere, even in England. This reaction will be a fine inheritance for my son. It is possible that the English, in order to efface the remembrance of their persecutions, will favour my son's return to France. But in order to live in a good understanding with England, it is necessary at any cost to favour her commercial interests. This necessity leads to one of these two consequences—war with England, or a sharing of the commerce of the world with her. This second condition is the only one possible in the present day. The exterior question will long take precedence in

France of the interior. I bequeath to my son sufficient strength and sympathy to enable him to continue my work with the single aid of an elevated and conciliatory diplomacy.

"His position at Vienna is deplorable. Will Austria set him at liberty unconditionally? But after all, Francis I. was once in a more critical position, and yet his French nationality was nothing impaired by it. Let not my son ever mount the throne by the aid of foreign influence. His aim should be not to fulfil a desire to reign, but to deserve the approbation of posterity. Let him cherish an intimacy with my family, whenever it shall be in his power. My mother is a woman of the old school. Joseph and Eugène are able to give him good counsel. Hortense and Catherine are superior women. If he remains in exile, let him marry one of my nieces. If France recalls him, let him seek the hand of a Princess of Russia. This court is the only one where family ties rule policy. The alliance which he may contract should tend to increase the exterior influence of France, and not to introduce a foreign influence into its councils. The French nation, when it is not taken the wrong way, is more easily governed than any other. Its prompt and easy comprehension is unequalled. It immediately discerns who labours for and who against it. But then it is necessary always to speak to its senses, otherwise its uneasy spirit gnaws; it explodes and ferments. My son will arrive after a time of civil troubles. He has but one party to fear, that of the Duke of Orleans. This party has been germinating for a long time. Let him despise all parties, and only see the mass of the people. Excepting those who have betrayed their country, he ought to forget the previous conduct of all men, and reward talent, merit, and services wherever he finds them. Chateaubriand, notwithstanding his libel, is a good Frenchman.

"France is the country where the chiefs of parties have the least influence. To rest for support on them is to build on sand. Great things can only be done in France by having the support of the *mass of the people*. Besides, a government should always seek support where it is really to be found. There are moral laws as inflexible and imperious as the physical ones. The Bourbons can only rely for support on the nobles and the priest, whatever may be the constitution which they are made to adopt. The water will descend again to its level, in spite of the machine which has raised it for a moment. I, on the contrary, relied on the whole mass of the people without exception. I set the example of a government which favoured the interests of all. I did not govern by the help of, or solely for either the nobles, the priests, the citizens, or tradesmen. I governed for the whole community, for the whole family of the French nation.

"My nobility will afford no support to my son. I required more than one generation to succeed in making them assume my colour, and preserve, by tradition, the sacred deposit of my moral conquests. From the year 1815, all the grandees openly espoused the opposite party. I felt no reliance either on my marshals or my nobility, not even on my colonels; but the whole mass of the people, and the whole army, up to the grade of captain, were on my side. I was not deceived in feeling this confidence. They owe much to me. I was their true representative. My dictatorship was indispensable. The proof of this is, that they always offered me more power than I desired. In the present day there is nothing possible in France but what is necessary. It will not be the same with my son. His power will be disputed. He must anticipate every desire for liberty. It is, besides, easier in ordinary times to reign with the help of the Chambers than alone. The Assemblies take a great part of your responsibility, and nothing is more easy than always to have the majority on your side; but care must be taken not to demoralise the country. The influence of the government in France is immense; and if it understands the way, it has no need of employing corruption in order to find support on all sides. The aim of a sovereign is not only to reign, but to diffuse instruction, morality, and well-being. Anything false is but a bad aid.

"In my youth, I too entertained some illusions; but I soon recovered from them. The great orators who rule the assemblies by the brilliance of their eloquence, are, in general, men of the most mediocre political talents. They should not be opposed in their own way, for they have always more noisy words at command than you. Their eloquence should be opposed by a serious and logical argument. Their strength lies in vagueness. They should be brought back to the reality of facts. Practical arguments destroy them. In the Council there were men possessed of much more eloquence than I was. I always defeated them by this simple argument—*two and two make four*.

"France possesses very clever practical men. The only thing necessary is to find them, and to give them the means of reaching the proper station. One is at the plough, who ought to be in the council, and another is minister who ought to be at the plough. Let not my son be astonished to hear men, the most reasonable to all appearance, propose to him the most absurd plans. From the agrarian law to the despotism of the Grand

Turk, every system finds an apologist in France. Let him listen to them all; let him take everything at its just value, and surround himself by all the real capacity of the country. The French people are influenced by two powerful passions—the love of liberty and the love of distinction. These, though seemingly opposed, are derived from one and the same feeling, a government can only satisfy these two wants by the most exact justice. The law and action of the government must be equal towards all. Honours and rewards must be conferred on the men who seem in the eyes of all to be most worthy of them. Merit may be pardoned, but not intrigue. The order of the Legion of Honour has been an immense and powerful incitement to virtue, talent, and courage. If ill employed, it would become a great evil by alienating the whole army, if the spirit of court intrigue and côterie presided at its nominations or in its administrations.

"My son will be obliged to allow the liberty of the press. This is a necessity in the present day. In order to govern, it is not necessary to pursue a more or less perfect theory, but to build with the materials which are under one's hand; to submit to necessities and profit by them. The liberty of the press ought to become, in the hands of the government, a powerful auxiliary in diffusing, through all the most distant corners of the empire, sound doctrines and good principles. To leave it to itself would be to fall asleep on the brink of a danger. On the conclusion of a general peace, I would have instituted a Directory of the Press, composed of the ablest men of the country; and I would have diffused, even to the most distant hamlet, my ideas and my intentions. In the present day it is impossible to remain as one might have done three hundred years ago—a quiet spectator of the transformations of society. Now one must, under the pain of death, either direct or hinder everything.

"My son ought to be a man of new ideas, and of the cause which I have made triumphant everywhere. He ought to establish institutions which shall efface all traces of the feudal law, secure the dignity of man, and develope those germs of prosperity which have been budding for centuries. He should propagate in all those countries uncivilized and barbarous, the benefits of Christianity and civilization. Such should be the aim of all my son's thoughts. Such is the cause for which I die a martyr to the hatred of the oligarchs, of which I am the object. Let him consider the holiness of my cause. Look at the regicides! They were formerly in the councils of a Bourbon. To-morrow they will return to their country, and I and mine expiate in torture the blessings which I desired to bestow on nations. My enemies are the enemies of humanity. They desire to fetter the people, whom they regard as a flock of sheep. They endeavour to oppress France, and to make the stream re-ascend towards its source. Let them take care that it does not burst its bounds.

"With my son, all opposite interests may live in peace; new ideas be diffused and gather strength, without any violent shock, or the sacrifice of any victims, and humanity be spared dreadful misfortunes. But if the blind hatred of kings still pursues my blood after my death, I shall then be avenged, but cruelly avenged. Civilization will suffer in every way, if nations burst their bounds, and rivers of blood will be shed throughout the whole of Europe; the lights of science and knowledge will be extinguished amid civil and foreign warfare. More than three hundred years of troubles will be required in order to destroy in Europe that royal authority which has, but for a day, represented the interests of all classes of men, but which struggled for several centuries before it could throw off all the restraints of the Middle Ages. If, on the other hand, the North advances against civilization, the struggle will be of shorter duration, but the blows more fatal. The well-being of nations, all the results which it has taken so many years to obtain, will be destroyed, and none can foresee the disastrous consequences. The accession of my son is for the interest of nations, as well as kings. Beyond the circle of ideas and principles for which we have fought, and which I have carried triumphantly through all difficulties, I see nought but slavery and confusion for France and for the whole of Europe.

"You will publish all that I have dictated or written, and you will engage my son to read and reflect upon it. You will tell him to protect all those who have served me well, and their number is large. My poor soldiers, so devoted, so magnanimous, are now, perhaps, in want of bread! What buried riches, which will, perhaps, never again see the light of day! Europe is progressing toward an inevitable transformation. To endeavour to retard this progress would be but to lose strength by a useless struggle. To favour it is to strengthen the hopes and wishes of all.

"There are desires of nationality which must be satisfied sooner or later. It is towards this end that continual progress should be made. My son's position will not be exempt from immense difficulties. Let him do by general consent what I was compelled by circumstances to effect by force of arms. When I was victorious over Russia, in 1812, the problem of a peace of a hundred years' duration was solved. I cut the Gordian knot of nations. In the present day it must be untied. The remembrance of the thrones which I raised up, when it was for the general interest of my policy so to do, should be effaced. In the year 1815, I exacted from my brothers that they should forget their royalty, and only take the title of French princes. My son should follow this example. An opposite course would excite just alarm.

"It is no longer in the North that great questions will be resolved, but in the Mediterranean. There, there is enough to content all the ambition of the different powers; and the happiness of civilized nations may be purchased with fragments of barbarous lands. Let the kings listen to reason. Europe will no longer afford matter for maintaining international hatreds. Prejudices are dissipated and intermingled. Routes of commerce are becoming multiplied. It is no longer possible for one nation to monopolize it. As a means by which my son may see whether his administration be good or the contrary, whether his laws are in accordance with the manners of the country, let him have an annual and particular report presented to him of the number of condemnations pronounced by the tribunals. If crimes and delinquencies increase in number, it is a proof that misery is on the increase, and that society is ill governed. Their diminution, on the other hand, is a proof of the contrary.

"Religious ideas have more influence than certain narrow-minded philosophers are willing to believe. They are capable of rendering great services to humanity. By standing well with the Pope an influence is still maintained over the consciences of a hundred millions of men. Pius VII. will be always well-disposed towards my son. He is a tolerant and enlightened old man. Fatal circumstances embroiled our cabinets; I regret this deeply. Cardinal Fesch did not understand me. He upheld the party of the *Ultramontanes*, the enemies of true religion in France. If you are permitted to return to France, you will still find many who have remained faithful to my memory. The best monuments which they could raise to me would be to make a collection of all the ideas which I expressed in the Council of State for the administration of the empire; to collect all my instructions to my ministers, and to make a list of the works which I undertook, which I raised in France and Italy. In what I have said in the Council of State, a distinction must be made, between the measures good only for the moment, and those the application of which is eternally true.

"Let my son often read and reflect on history. This is the only true philosophy. Let him read and meditate on the wars of the greatest captains. This is the only means of rightly learning the science of war. But all that you say to him, or all that he learns will be of little use to him if he has not in the depth of his heart that sacred fire and love of good which alone can effect great things. I will hope, however, that he will be worthy of his destiny."

"I had," said Napoleon to Dr. Arnott, "come to seek the hospitality of the British people; I asked for a generous protection, and to the subversion of every right held sacred upon earth, chains were the reply I received. I should have experienced a different reception from Alexander. . . . . Your ministers have chosen this horrible rock, upon which the lives of Europeans are exhausted in less than three years, in order to end my existence by . . . . And how have I been treated since my arrival here? There is no species of indignity or insult that has not been eagerly heaped upon me. The simplest family communications, which have never been interdicted to any one, have been refused to me. No news, no papers from Europe have been allowed to reach me; my wife and son have no longer existed for me: I have been kept six years in the tortures of close confinement. The most uninhabitable spot on this inhospitable island, that where the murderous effects of a tropical climate are most severely felt, has been assigned to me for a residence, and I, who used to ride on horseback all over Europe, have been obliged to shut myself up within four walls, in an unwholesome atmosphere. I have been destroyed piecemeal by a premeditated and protracted . . . and the . . . Hudson has been the executer of the high deeds and exploits of your ministers. . . . You will end like the proud republic of Venice; and I dying upon this dreary rock, away from those I hold dear, and deprived of everything, bequeath the opprobrium and horror of my death to the reigning family of England."

Napoleon often nursed little Napoleon Bertrand, when he would say, "If my son were with me!" then he added, "I should not be happier, he would console me for a time, but when I thought of his future—"

Of Pope's Iliad, Napoleon said, "This is the proof that of all languages the English most nearly resembles the Greek. Pope, of all authors is the one who has best translated Homer."

In conversation with an English general, Napoleon spoke of General Monk's restoration of the throne to Charles II. When I took the reins of the French government," he said, " my political situation was very different to that of Monk; England, at the death of Cromwell, was divided into different parties, but it was outwardly peaceable. Richard, his son, did not know how to profit by the labours of his father, and the majority recalled Charles to the throne. When the general was gone, Napoleon was heard to say to himself aloud, " When the advocate, Gohier, the apostate Sieyes, the procurer Rewbel, and Moulins had made themselves kings, I might well make myself consul. I had taken out my licences at Montenotte, at Lodi Arcola, and Aboukir.

When Captain Poppleton took leave of Napoleon at St. Helena, the ex-emperor offered him a snuff-box set with diamonds, saying to him, " Adieu! my friend, this is the only trifle which remains to me. I present it to you in order that you may, after my death, show this pledge of my gratitude."

" I shall rejoin my brave companions in the Elysian fields. Yes, Kleber, Dessaix, Bessière, Duroc, Ney, Murat, Massena, Berthier will come to greet me, and to talk with me of what we have done together. I shall recount to them the latest events of my life. On seeing me they will rekindle with enthusiasm and glory, and we will discourse of our wars and glory with the Scipios, the Hannibals, with Cæsar and with Frederick. There will be pleasure in that, unless (smiling) they should be alarmed below to see so many warriors assembled together."

About ten days before his death Napoleon asked for a newspaper. One was procured, and running his eyes over it he exclaimed, "Naples, Naples; poor devil! Murat was the best king they have ever had; but he did not know his subjects. From the duke of Calabria to the lowest beggar, they are all Lazzaroni.* The old king is . . . Have you been to Naples, sir?"

"Yes, sire."

"Ah! beautiful women, well-made men, and—and—they understand the art of being happy."

A few days afterwards, he said softly, "I should like to have seen my wife and son again, but God's will be done."

The evening before his death he spoke more than ordinary, and hummed his favourite air—

"O Richard, ô mon roi,
 L'univers t'abandonne."

On the morning before his death he said, "There is nothing terrible in death; he has been by my pillow for the last three weeks, and now he is about to take me away for ever."

---

* "From this courteous but kind-hearted man of letters (Professor Ebeling), I heard a tolerable Italian pun and an interesting anecdote. When Bonaparte was in Italy, having been irritated by some instance of perfidy, he said in a loud and vehement tone, in a public company: ''Tis a true proverb—*Gli Italiani ladroni,*' i. e. the Italians all plunderers. A lady had the courage to reply, '*Non tutti; ma buona parte.*' [Not all, but a good part, or Buonaparte]. This I confess sounded to my ears one of the many good things that *might* have been said."—*Coleridge's Biographia Literaria,* p. 255.

The last words that Napoleon was heard to pronounce were " My God ! . . And the French nation . . My son . . Head army . . France ! France.*

---

* One cannot tell what connection these two words, *Head army*, could have in his mind, but they were distinctly heard, about seven o'clock in the morning. Some moments after, he said, " France ! France." These were his last words. He breathed his last sigh on Saturday, the 5th of May, 1821, at twenty minutes to six in the evening.—" *Les trois derniers Mois de la Vie de l'Empéreur Napoléon.*

APHORISMS.*

FRIENDSHIP is but a name.

The only victory over love is flight.

Great ambition is the passion of a great character. He who is endowed with it may perform either very great or very bad actions; all depends upon the principles which direct him.

Love does more harm than good.

The heart may be broken, and the soul remain unshaken.

Great reserve and severity of manners are necessary for the command of those who are older than ourselves.

Flatterers and learned men do not agree together.

There is glory and true greatness in raising one's self by the heart.

Passionate people always deny their anger, and cowards often boast their ignorance of fear.

There are calumnies against which even innocence loses courage.

---

* Some of Napoleon's aphorisms it is impossible or unnecessary to find a date for. We have, therefore, thought it better to place them at the end, avoiding as much as possible a repetition of those phrases which have been already given in his conversations and letters.

He who is unmoved by tears has no heart.

The sight of a battle-field after the fight, is enough to inspire princes with a love of peace and a horror of war.

It is the cause, and not the death that makes the martyr.

Military bravery has nothing in common with civil courage.

The conscience is the inviolable asylum of the liberty of man.

Words pass away, but actions remain.

Grief has its bounds, which must not be exceeded.

All predictions are impostures, the result of fraud, folly, or fanaticism.

I failed; therefore, according to all justice I was wrong.

Experience is the true wisdom of nations.

Greatness is nothing, unless it be lasting.

The best way to cure the body is to quiet the mind.

Fortune has always been the first title to consideration.

Girls cannot be better brought up than by their mother; public education is not suitable to them.

There is no more fatal misfortune for a man than to allow himself to be governed by his wife; in such case he is neither himself nor his wife; he is simply nothing.

In great crises it is women's lot to soften our misfortunes.

Fanaticism must be lulled first, in order that it may be uprooted.

Nothing is done while something still remains to be done.

The woman we love is always the most beautiful of her sex.

When firmness is sufficient, rashness is unnecessary.

Great men are those who can control both good luck and fortune.

He who fears being conquered is sure of defeat.

The greater the man, the less will should he have; he depends on circumstances and events.

Better never to have been born than to live without glory.

It is never wise to inflame hatred, nor to render one's self odious.

A true man hates no one.

It is in times of difficulty that great men and great nations display all the energy of their character, and become an object of admiration to posterity.

We must laugh at man, to avoid crying for him.

Where flowers degenerate man cannot live.

Men are not so ungrateful as they are said to be. If they are often complained of, it generally happens that the benefactor exacts more than he has given.

Men have their virtues, their vices, their heroism, their perverseness; they possess and exercise all that is good, and all that is bad in this world.

Men, in general, are but great children.

Men of letters are useful men who should ever be distinguished, as they do honour to their country.

Disdain hatreds; hear both sides, and delay judgment until reason has had time to resume her sway.

Great men are like meteors, which shine and consume themselves to enlighten the earth.

Historians are like the sheep of Panurge, they copy that which their predecessors have written, so that their opinions and interest are not opposed to it, without troubling themselves to inquire into truth or even probabilities.

Indecision and anarchy in leaders lead to weakness and anarchy in results.

Independence, like honour, is a rocky island, without a beach.

Uncertainty is painful for all nations and for all men.

When we have drunk the cup of pleasure to the dregs, all we want is rest.

Judgment in extreme cases should be guided by precedent.

We can only escape the arbitrariness of the judge by placing ourselves under the despotism of the law.

To really understand a man, we must judge him in misfortune.

Liberty and equality are magical words.

The only encouragement for literature is to give the poet a position in the state.

The praises of an enemy are suspicious: they cannot flatter a man of honour until after the cessation of hostilities.

We should wash our dirty linen at home.*

We are strong, when we have made up our minds to die.

We walk faster when we walk alone.

Death may expiate faults, but it does not repair them.

Man is ever ready to forsake the wonders which surround him for the wonders that others point out; for everything about us is wonderful.

We are all destined to die! Can a few days of life equal the happiness of dying for one's country?

Misfortunes have their heroism and their glory.

There is nothing terrible in death.

Marriage has always been the conclusion of love.

Death overtakes the coward; but never the brave man till his hour is come.

---

* *Il faut laver son linge sale en famille.* A common French Proverb.

As the basis of our decision for marrying a woman, we should consider her moral qualifications, such as gentleness, economy, and capacity for the management of a family. These qualities are the fundamental principles of matrimony.

The beauties of the Venus de Medicis are only secondary qualifications in marriage.

Pride never listens to the voice of reason, nature, or religion.

Peace is the first of necessities, and the first of glories.

A priest should never throw off his cassock: he should never for one moment hide his real character.

The problems of Providence are insoluble.

When a man is determined to hold a place (under government), he has already sold himself to it.

Paradise is a central spot, where the souls of all mankind arrive by different roads; each sect has its own particular path.

Wisdom demands forethought.

Chance is the providence of adventurers.

It is unjust, odious, and impolitic, to punish a son for the faults of his father, and to deprive him of his inheritance.

There is a similarity of position as regards religion and kings—each may be dethroned.

True wisdom, in general, consists in energetic determination.

It is as necessary for the heart to feel, as for the body to be fed.

The sympathies of a tottering nation can add no strength to an army.

We must use water, not oil, to quench theological volcanoes.

A glutton will defend his food like a hero.

Power is founded upon opinion.

True civil liberty consists in the security of property.

Men are led by trifles.

Public instruction should be the first object of government.

Public esteem is the reward of honest men.

We must either strike or be stricken.

The government of many is anarchy.

Cruelty can only be justified by necessity.

The most trifling circumstances produce the greatest results.

A minister of state should never allow a woman to approach his cabinet.

Frenchmen know not how to form conspiracies.

The world must be governed without regard to individual actions.

A military government is favourable to royal authority.

A prince casts liberty aside when it throws impediments in his path.

I command or I am silent.

It is not easy to check the people when they are once set in motion.

In politics, there is a wide gulf between promises and performances.

In politics, family considerations are absurd.

The police invents more than it discovers.

The best policy is simplicity and truth.

Revolutions are like the most noxious dung-heaps, which bring into life the noblest vegetables.

A treaty not ratified within the prescribed time, has no positive existence.

It is easier to brave and threaten than to conquer.

The will of princes is sometimes foiled; it depends upon events, and awaits their issue.

The throne is but a bit of gilded wood covered with velvet.

In a monarchy, the throne and the person of the king are inseparable.

NOTES.

Note 1.

NAPOLEON BONAPARTE was born at Ajaccio, in Corsica, on the 15th of August, 1769; the old orthography of his name was Buonaparte, but he suppressed the *u* during his first campaign in Italy. His motives for so doing were merely to render the spelling conformable with the pronunciation, and to abridge his signature.—*Bourrienne's Memoirs of Bonaparte.*

2. "Incapable to estimate his uncommon merit, or rather, to penetrate his true motives, his superiors and schoolfellows taxed him with being foolish and ridiculous. Every means was tried, but in vain, to restore him to himself by making him change his conduct. Insensible to affronts which he could not resent, he repelled the railleries of the masters by silence and disdain. Humiliation and even punishment, which were also employed, had no better success."—*The Entertaining History of the Early Years of General Bonaparte. By a Royal Emigrant, one of Bonaparte's Schoolfellows.* (1810.)

3. Josephine de Beauharnais was a native of St. Domingo, and the daughter of a planter named De la Pagerie. While she was an infant, she herself stated, a negro sorceress prophesied that "she should one day be greater than a queen, and yet outlive her dignity." According to some, the last clause ran, "die in an hospital," which was in the sequel interpreted to mean Malmaison—a palace which (like our own St. James's) had once been an hospital.

4. Before Madame Beauharnais' marriage with Bonaparte she wrote to a friend as follows:—" I admire the General's courage; the extent of his knowledge on every subject (for on every one he speaks equally well); the penetration of his mind which enables him to apprehend another's thought almost before it is expressed; but I own I am not without dread on beholding the empire which he appears to exercise over everything around him. His scrutinizing look has in it something singular—something which I cannot explain, but which is felt even by our directors. Must it not, then, intimidate a woman? Barras tells me, that if I marry the General, he shall have the chief command of the army of Italy. Yesterday, in speaking of this promotion, which though not yet bestowed, causes his brother officers to murmur, Bonaparte said to me,—' Do they (the Directors) believe that I stand in need of PROTECTION to make my way? Some time all of them will be happy to receive *mine!* I wear a sword, which will be found my best patron.' What think you of this certainty of success? Is it not a proof of overweening confidence, proceeding from excessive self-love? A general of brigade protect the heads of government! After all, it is likely enough. Sometimes this ridiculous assurance imposes on me to such a degree that I believe possible whatever this extraordinary man may take a fancy to attempt; and with his imagination, who can say what he may *not* attempt?"—*Mémoires de Josephine.* Paris, 1829.

[Bourrienne pronounces this work *genuine, though published anonymously.*]

5. Josephine was remarkable for her extravagance. On one occasion she owed no less than 1,200,000 francs, and prevailed upon the secretary to state her debts at half that sum. "The anger of the First Consul," says Bourrienne, "may be conceived. He suspected, however, that his wife concealed something; but he said,—' Take the 600,000 francs, but let that sum suffice; let me be pestered with no more of her debts. Threaten the creditors with the loss of their accounts if they do not renounce their enormous profits.' These accounts Madame Bonaparte laid before me. The exorbitant price of every article arising from the fear of the creditors either that they must give very long credit, or in the end be

compelled to make a considerable abatement is incredible. I thought, too, that many articles were charged for which had never been delivered. In one bill, for instance, thirty-eight hats of a very high price were supplied in one month; the feathers alone were 1,800 francs. I asked Josephine if she wore two hats a day, she said, 'It must be an error.' Other overcharges, both as to the price, and the things furnished, evinced the same system of plunder. I followed the Consul's advice, and spared neither reproaches nor threats. I am ashamed to say that the greater number of the tradesmen were satisfied with one-half of their bills; one of them consented to receive 35,000 francs instead of 80,000, and had the impudence to boast before my face that he had a good profit left."

6. "The First Consul, being informed that the carriers of the mails conveyed also a variety of other things, especially delicacies for certain favoured persons, ordered that in future the service of the post should be confined to letters and despatches. That very evening Cambacères entered the room in which I was sitting with the First Consul, who enjoyed beforehand the embarrassment of his colleague. 'Well, Cambacères, what is the matter at this hour?' 'I come to request an exception to the order you have given to the director of the posts. How do you suppose that friends can either be made or preserved without the best dishes? You know yourself that a good table has a great deal to do with the art of governing.' The First Consul laughed heartily, called him a gourmand, and patting him on the shoulder said,—'Be comforted, my poor Cambacères, forget your anger; the couriers shall continue to bring your patés de Strasbourg.'"—*Bourrienne's Memoirs.*

7. "Bonaparte," says Madame de Staël, "chose with singular sagacity for his assistant consuls, two men who were of no use but to disguise the unity of his despotism. The one was Cambacères, a lawyer of great learning, who had been taught in the Convention to bend methodically before terror; the other Lebrun, a man of highly cultivated mind and highly polished manners, who had been trained under the Chancellor Maupeou —under that minister who, satisfied with the degree of arbi-

trary power which he found in the monarchy as it then existed, had substituted for the parliaments of France one named by himself. Cambacères was the interpreter of Bonaparte to the revolutionists; Lebrun to the royalists. Both translated the same text into two different languages. Thus two able ministers were charged with the task of adapting the old system and the new to the mixed mass of the third. The one a great noble, who had been engaged in the revolution, told the royalists that it was their interest to recover monarchical institutions, at the expense of renouncing the ancient dynasty. The other, who, though a creature of the era of disaster, was ready to promote the re-establishment of courts, preached to the republicans the necessity of abandoning their political opinions in order to preserve their places."

8. The following is a tolerable example of the system of espionage pursued by Savary:—

A man who had lost his two sons in the Russian campaign was suspected of not being very heartily attached to the existing government; such, indeed, was the fact, but he was prudent enough to speak his mind only in presence of his most intimate friends; before the rest of the world he was mute, thereby baffling the efforts of the numerous hired spies whom Savary had placed over him. As he was one day seated in the garden of the Luxembourg, accompanied by a tried friend, the conversation began with the battle of Leipsic, which had recently taken place. In the sequel neither spared the despot, whose downfal they hoped was near at hand. In the midst of this confidential intercourse a lovely little boy, apparently in his sixth year, came weeping towards them, crying that he had lost his nurse. They endeavoured to comfort him, telling him not to sob, for his nurse would not fail to seek him. During the quarter of an hour which he remained with them they continued to converse on the same subject. Then a woman was seen to approach with a child in her arms; no sooner did the boy perceive her than he cried, "There is my nurse," and hastened to rejoin her. The very next morning both were arrested and conducted to the Conciergerie. The childless parent was the first interrogated, and his surprise was not little to hear repeated, word for word, a portion of his conversation with his friend. His natural impression was that that friend had betrayed him, but he soon found his mistake. Both were immediately imprisoned, nor were they enlarged before the fall of Napoleon. Children of both sexes were employed in this execrable system of espionage.—*Court and Camp of Bonaparte.*

9. Not even Napoleon's example could persuade the Parisians to wear ill-shaped hats and clumsy boots; but he in his own person adhered to the last to his original connection with these poor artisans.

10. The following list of books for a Camp Library Napoleon made out with his own hand, before the expedition to the East:—

I. *Science and the Arts.*—Plurality of Worlds, Fontenelle, 1 vol. Letters to a German Princess, 2 vols. Course of the Normal School, 6 vols. Treatise on Artillery, 1 vol. On Fortifications, 3 vols. On Fireworks, 1 vol.

II. *Geography and Travels.*—Barclay's Geography, 12 vols. Cook's Voyages, 3 vols. La Harpe's Collection of French Voyages and Travels, 24 vols.

III. *History.*—Plutarch, 12 vols. Turenne, 2 vols. Condé, 4 vols. Villars, 4 vols. Luxembourg, 2 vols. Duguesclin, 2 vols. Saxe, 3 vols. Memoirs of the French Marshals, 20 vols. President Hainault, 4 vols. Chronology, 2 vols. Marlborough, 4 vols. Prince Eugène, 6 vols. Philosophical History of India, 12 vols. Germany, 2 vols. Charles XII., 1 vol. Essay on the Manners of Nations, 6 vols. Peter the Great, 1 vol. Polybius, 6 vols. Justin, 2 vols. Arrian, 3 vols. Tacitus, 2 vols. Livy, — vols. Thucydides, 2 vols. Vertot, 4 vols. Deuina, 8 vols. Frederic II., 8 vols.

IV. *Poetry.*—Ossian, 1 vol. Tasso, 6 vols. Ariosto, 6 vols. Homer, 6 vols. Virgil, 4 vols. Henriade, 1 vol. Télémaque, 2 vols. The Gardens (Delille) 1 vol. Masterpieces of the French Drama, 20 vols. Select Fugitive Poetry, 10 vols. La Fontaine, — vols.

V. *Fiction.*—Voltaire, 4 vols. Heloise, 4 vols. Werther, 1 vol. Marmontel, 4 vols. English Novels, 40 vols. Le Sage, 10 vols. Prevost, 10 vols.

VI. *Political* (?)—Old Testament and New. The Koran.

The Vedane. Mythology. Montesquieu. Spirit of Laws. In a note to this, Dr. Memes, the translator of the Edinburgh edition (1831) of Bourrienne's Memoirs, says very justly. "There appears a sad affectation in the title and contents of the last division of this list, and the whole shows shallow acquirement, and in some instances bad taste. The scientific portion, especially the mathematical, will astonish those readers who know the subject."

11. In the expedition to Egypt, the common men beheld with no friendly eye the troop of *savans* mounted on asses (the common conveyance of the country), with all their instruments, books, and baggage. They began to suspect that the expedition had been undertaken for some merely scientific purposes, and when on any alarm they were ordered to open the square and give the learned party safe footing within, they used to receive them with military jeerings, "room for the asses: stand back, here come the *savans* and the *demi-savans*."

12. *Respect for the ceremonies of the Koran.* Napoleon held a conversation as follows, in one of the pyramids with several Imams and Muftis who accompanied him. It may amuse by its singurality:

Bonaparte. God is great, and his works are marvellous. Here is a great work from the hands of man. What was the object of the man who built this pyramid?

Suleiman. He was a great and powerful king of Egypt, whose name we believe to be Cheops. He wished that no sacrilege should disturb the repose of his ashes.

Bonaparte. The great Cyrus was buried in the open air, so that his body should return to its elements. Do you not think he did better? do you think so?

Suleiman (bowing), Glory to God, to whom all glory is due!

Bonaparte. Honour to Allah! What caliph opened this pyramid and disturbed the repose of the dead?

Muhamed. It is believed by some the Commander of the Faithful, who reigned many ages ago at Bagdad; others say the renowned Haroun al Raschid (God rest his soul), who thought to find treasure there; but when the pyramid was entered by his orders, tradition says that only mummies were found, and upon the wall this inscription in letters of gold:

"The impious will commit sin without result, but not without remorse."

Bonaparte. The bread stolen by the wicked, fills his mouth with gravel.

Muhamed (bowing), It is the discourse of wisdom.

Bonaparte. Glory to Allah! there is no God but God; Mahomet is his prophet, and I am one of his friends.

Suleiman. Peace to the one sent of God. Health also to thee, invincible general, favourite of Mahommed.

Bonaparte. Mufti, I thank thee. The divine Koran is the delight of my soul and the attention of my eyes. I love the prophet, and I hope before long to see and honour his tomb in the sacred city. But my mission henceforth is to exterminate the Mamelukes.

Ibrahim. May the angels of victory sweep the dust from thy path, and cover it with their wings. The Mameluke has deserved death.

Bonaparte. He has been stricken and given up to the black angels Moukir and Quakir. God, on whom all depends, has ordered that his dominion shall be destroyed.

Suleiman. He stretched out the hand of plunder over the lands, the crops and the horses of Egypt.

Bonaparte. And upon the most beautiful slaves, very holy Mufti. Allah has withered his hand. God is just and merciful to the people.

Ibrahim. O the most valiant amongst the children of Issa (Jesus Christ), Alla has made thee follow the exterminating angel to deliver his land of Egypt.

Bonaparte. This land was given up to twenty-four oppressors, rebels to the great Sultan our ally (whom God surround with glory), and to 10,000 slaves from Canada and Georgia; Adriel, angel of death, has breathed upon them; we have come, and they have disappeared.

Muhamed. Noble successor of Scander (Alexander), honour to thy invincible arms, and to the unexpected thunder that proceeds from the midst of thy warlike horsemen.

Bonaparte. Do you know that that thunder is a work of the children of men? Allah put it into my hands by the genius of war.

Ibrahim. We recognize in thy works Allah who sends thee. Wouldst thou be a conqueror if Allah did not permit it? The Delta and all the neighbouring countries resound with thy miracles.

Bonaparte. A celestial chariot (a balloon) shall rise by my orders to the dwelling-place of the clouds, and the thunder shall descend to the earth by a thread of metal (a lightning conductor), as soon as I shall have commanded it.

Suleiman. And the great serpent fell from the column of Pompey on the day of thy triumphant entry to Alexandria, and has remained dry upon the pedestal, is not that a wonder produced by thy hand?

Bonaparte. Lights of the age, you are destined to see still greater wonders, for the days of regeneration are come.

Ibrahim. The Divine Unity looks at thee with an eye of predilection, adorer of Issa, and gives thee the support of the children of the prophet.

Bonaparte. Has not Mahomet said, *Every man who adores God and does good works, whatever may be his religion, shall be saved?*

Suleiman, Muhamed, Ibrahim (bowing), He has said it.

Bonaparte. And if by an order from on high, I have tempered the pride of the Vicar of Issa, by lessening his earthly possessions to amass celestial treasures for him, say, am I not giving glory to God whose mercy is infinite?

Muhamed (with embarrassment). The Mufti of Rome was rich and powerful, but we are only poor Muftis.

Bonaparte. I know it. Do not fear. You have been weighed in the balance of Balthazard, and you have been found wanting. . . This pyramid did not contain any treasure that was known to you then?

Suleiman. No sire. We swear it by the holy city of Mecca.

Bonaparte. Cursed, thrice cursed be those who seek for perishable riches, and heap up gold and silver like mud.

Suleiman. Thou hast spared the Vicar of Issa, and treated him with clemency and goodness.

Bonaparte. He is an old man whom I honour (may God give him his desires when they shall be regulated by reason and truth), but he has condemned all Mussulmans to eternal fire; and Allah condemns intolerance in all.

Ibrahim. Glory to Allah and to his prophet, who has sent thee into the midst of us to rekindle the faith of the weak, and open to the faithful the doors of the seventh heaven.

Bonaparte. You have said it, very zealous Muftis. Be faithful to Allah, the sovereign master of the seven marvellous heavens; to Mahomet, who traversed all the heavens in a night. Be friends of the Franks, and Allah, Mahomet and the Franks will reward you.

Ibrahim. May the prophet himself give thee to sit at his left hand on the resurrection day, after the third sound of the trumpet.

Bonaparte. He who has ears to hear, let him hear; the hour of resurrection has arrived for all people labouring under oppression. Muftis, Imams, Mullahs, Dervishes, Kalenders, instruct the people of Egypt; encourage them to join us in weakening the Beys and the Mamelukes; look favourably upon the commerce of France in your countries. The treasures, the industry, and the friendship of the Franks shall be yours till you mount to the seventh heaven, and seated by the side of the black-eyed houris, always virgins and always young, you repose under the shade of the Lama, whose branches will offer to the true Mussulmans all that they can desire.

Suleiman. Thou hast spoken like the most learned of the Mullahs. We place faith in thy words; we will serve thy cause, and God hears us.

Bonaparte. God is great, and His works are marvellous. Peace be upon you, most holy Muftis.

Madame de Staël says of this conversation:

It ought to enchant the Parisians, because it unites the two qualities most captivating to them; a certain species of greatness, and of mockery at the same time. The French are very easily moved; charlatanism pleases them, and they willingly help to deceive themselves provided they are permitted all the while they are acting like dupes, to prove by *bon mots* that they are nevertheless not so.

13. "It was said of Murat by Napoleon that when he advanced to the charge he resembled a paladin of old more than a modern soldier. In his costume he imitated the ancient knights; his noble port showed majestically under the chivalric

garb; add to this his more than mortal daring, and we shall not wonder that the very Cossacks raised a shout of admiration when he approached them. A striking example of this occurred September 4th. The king with a few squadrons had left Giatz, followed at some distance by the grand army; in his march he was much annoyed by clouds of Cossacks who hovered about the heads of his columns, and from time to time compelled them to deploy. This troublesome series of interruptions at length incensed him to such a degree that he galloped up to them unattended, and in an authoritative voice cried out 'Clear the way, vermin!' It is a fact equally extraordinary and incontestable that these wild sons of the desert were so awed by his manner, as involuntarily to obey his command, nor did they again block up the way during the whole of that day's march."—*Court and Camp of Bonaparte.*

14. At Eylau the French army was in a critical situation. Augereau had been routed, the march of Davoust had been impeded, Ney and Bernadotte were at a distance; and the Emperor was so much discouraged at the heavy loss he had sustained, that he wished to fall back to effect a junction with his other corps.

"'Beware of doing so, sire!' exclaimed Soult with vivacity. 'Let us remain the last on the field, and we shall have the honour of the day. From what I have seen, I suspect the enemy will retreat during the night.' The Emperor complied with his marshal's suggestion, the wisdom of which was fully justified by the event, and he was soon rewarded with the ducal fief of Dalmatia."—*Court and Camp of Bonaparte.*

15. As a proof of Napoleon's constancy, it may be mentioned that Napoleon, when he had become great and illustrious, employed the same tradespeople, however inferior in their several crafts, who had served him in the days of his obscurity. A silversmith who had given him credit when he set out to Italy for a dressing-case worth £50, was rewarded with all the business which the recommendation of his now illustrious debtor could bring to him; and being clever in his trade became ultimately, under the patronage of the imperial household, one of the wealthiest citizens of Paris. A little hatter and a cobbler who had served Bonaparte when a subaltern

might have risen in the same manner had their skill equalled the silversmith's.

16. Cardinal Fesch appealed to the Emperor to try and divert him from the war with Russia on other grounds than those which Fouché suggested. The cardinal had been greatly afflicted by Napoleon's treatment of the pope, and he contemplated this new war with dread, as likely to bring down the vengeance of heaven on the head of one who had dared to trample on its vicegerent. He besought Napoleon not to provoke at once the wrath of man and the fury of the elements; and expressed his belief that he must one day sink under the weight of that universal hatred with which his actions were surrounding his throne. Bonaparte led the churchman to the window, opened it, and pointing upwards said, "Do you see yonder star?" "No sire," replied the cardinal. "But I see it," answered Napoleon, and abruptly dismissed him.

17. On the 24th of June the grand imperial army, consolidated into three masses, began the passage of the Niemen; the King of Westphalia at Grodno; the Viceroy Eugene at Pilony, and Napoleon himself near Kowno. The Emperor rode on in front of his army to reconnoitre the banks; his horse stumbled and he fell to the ground. "A bad omen, a Roman would return," some one exclaimed; who, it is not certain. The first party crossing was challenged by a single Cossack. "For what purpose," said he, "do you enter the Russian country?" "To beat you and take Wilna," answered the advanced guard. The sentinel struck spurs into his horse and disappeared in the forest. There came on at the same moment a tremendous thunder-storm. Thus began the fatal invasion.

18. During the invasion of Russia, there had been slain in battle on Napoleon's side 125,000 men. Fatigue, hunger, and cold had caused the death of 132,000; and the Russians had taken 193,000 prisoners, including forty-eight generals, and 3,000 regimental officers. The total loss, therefore, was 450,000 men. The eagles and standards left in the enemies' hands were seventy-five in number, and the pieces of cannon nearly one thousand. Exclusive of the Austrian and Prussian auxiliaries there remained of all the enormous host which Na-

poleon set in motion in August, about 40,000 men; and of these not 10,000 were of the French nation.

19. Hoffman describes Napoleon at the battle of Dresden, as coming on "with the eye of a tyrant and the voice of a lion urging his breathless and eager soldiers."

20. "Having myself long studied the 'man of destiny,' I have remarked that that which he called his fortune was in fact his genius; that his good luck resulted from his keen insight into things; from the calculations he made rapid as lightning; from the simultaneousness of his actions, and of his conceptions; and from the conviction which he himself cherished, that boldness is often wisdom."—*Bourrienne's Memoirs of Bonaparte.*

21. Napoleon, if we may believe Madame de Staël, had the weakness to affect in many trivial matters, a close imitation of what his new attendants reported to have been the personal demeanour of the Bourbon princes. His behaviour as the holder of a court was never graceful. He could not or would not control the natural vehemence of his temper, and ever and anon confounded the old race of courtiers by ebullitions which were better suited to the camp than the saloons of the Tuileries; but whenever he thought fit to converse with a man capable of understanding him, the Consul failed not to create a very lively feeling in his own favour; and meantime Josephine was admirably adapted to supply his deficiencies in the management of circles and festivals.

22. With regard to Napoleon's reclamations against the decision of the English government, it may probably suffice *now* to observe: 1st, That the government had never at any period acknowledged him as Emperor of France, and that it refused to be a party to the treaty under which he retired to Elba, simply because it was resolved not to acknowledge him as Emperor of Elba. These things Napoleon well knew, and as to his recent re-exercise of imperial functions in France, he well knew that the English government had continued to acknowledge Louis XVIII. as king all through the hundred days. Upon no principle, therefore, could he have expected beforehand to be treated as emperor by the ministers of the Prince Regent, nor even if he had been born a legitimate prince,

would it have been in the usual course of things for him, under existing circumstances, to persist in the open retention of his imperial style. By assuming some *incognito* as sovereigns when travelling out of their own dominions are accustomed to do, Napoleon might have cut the root away from one long series of his subsequent disputes with the English government and authorities. But in doing as he did, he acted on calculation. He never laid aside the hopes of escape and empire. It was his business to have complaints. If everything went on quietly and smoothly about him, what was to ensure the keeping up of a lively interest in his fortunes among the faction to which he still looked as inclined to befriend him, and above all among the soldiery, of whose personal devotion, even after the catastrophe of Waterloo, he had no reason to doubt? Bonaparte in his days of success always attached more importance to etiquette than a prince born to the purple and not quite a fool, would have been likely to do; but in the obstinacy with which after his total downfall, he clung to the airy sound of majesty, and such pigmy toys of observance as could be obtained under his circumstances, we cannot persuade ourselves to behold more than the sickly profession of a *parvenu*. The English government acknowledged him by the highest military rank he had held at the time when the treaty of Amiens was concluded with him as first consul; and the sound of General Bonaparte now so hateful in his ears who had under that style wielded the destinies of the world, might have been lost, if Napoleon himself had chosen, in some factitious style.

23. At Lodi Bonaparte himself appeared in the midst of the fire, pointing with his own hand two guns in such a manner as to cut off the Austrians from the only path by which they could have advanced to undermine the bridge; and it was on this occasion that the soldiery, delighted with his dauntless exposure of his person, conferred on him his honorary nickname of *the little corporal*. In the meantime he had sent General Beaumont and the cavalry to attempt the passage of the river by a distant ford (which they had much difficulty in effecting) and awaited with anxiety the moment when they should appear on the enemy's flank. When that took place Beaulieu's

line, of course, showed some confusion, and Napoleon instantly gave the word. A column of grenadiers whom he had kept ready drawn up close to the bridge, but under shelter of the houses, were in a moment wheeled to the left, and their leading files placed on the bridge. They rushed on shouting "*Vive la Republique*," but the storm of grape-shot for a moment checked them. Bonaparte, Lannes, Berthier and Lallemagne, hurried to the front, and rallied and cheered the men. The column dashed across the bridge in despite of the tempest of fire that thinned it. The brave Lannes was the first who reached the other side, Napoleon the second. The Austrian artillerymen were bayonetted at their guns ere the other troops whom Beaulieu had removed too far back in his anxiety to avoid the French battery, could come to their assistance. Beaulieu pressing gallantly with his horse upon the flank, and Napoleon's infantry forming rapidly as they passed the bridge, and charging on the instant, the Austrian line became involved in inextricable confusion, broke up and fled. The slaughter on their side was great; on the French there fell 200 men. With such rapidity, and consequently with so little loss, did Bonaparte execute this dazzling adventure "the terrible passage," as he himself called it "of the bridge of Lodi."

24. The battle of Roveredo is one of Napoleon's most illustrious days. The enemy had a strongly entrenched camp in front of the town; and behind it in case of misfortune, Calliano, with its castle seated on a precipice over the Adige, where that river flows between enormous rocks and mountains, appeared to offer an impregnable retreat. Nothing could withstand the ardour of the French. The Austrians, though they defended the intrenched camp with their usual obstinacy, were forced to give way by the impetuosity of Dubois and his hussars. Dubois fell, mortally wounded in the moment of his glory; he waved his sabre cheering his men onwards with his last breath. "I die," said he, "for the Republic, only let me hear, ere life leaves me, that the victory is ours." The French horse, thus animated, pursued the Germans, who were driven, unable to rally, through and beyond the town. Even the gigantic defences of Calliano proved of no avail.

Height after height was carried at the point of the bayonet; 7,000 prisoners and fifteen cannon remained with the conquerors. The Austrians fled to Levisa, which guards one of the chief defiles of the Tyrolese Alps, and were there beaten again. Vaubois occupied this important position with the gallant division who had forced it. Massena fixed himself in Wurmser's late head-quarters at Trent; and Napoleon having thus totally cut off the field-marshal's communication with Germany, proceeded to issue proclamations calling on the inhabitants of the Tyrol to receive the French as friends, and seize the opportunity of freeing themselves for ever from the dominion of Austria. He put forth an edict declaring that the sovereignty of the district was henceforth in the French Republic, and inviting the people themselves to arrange, according to their pleasure, its interior government.

25. Longwood is situated in the middle of a plain on the top of a mountain nearly eighteen hundred feet above the level of the sea and including Deadwood, occupies about fourteen or fifteen hundred acres of ground, of which a great part is planted with an indigenous tree called gumwood. Its appearance is sombre and monotonous. However, Napoleon preferred to fix his residence there, rather than in the town, where he would be incessantly exposed to the curious importunity of the inhabitants. Unfortunately the house only consisted of five rooms on the ground floor, which had been built one after the other acording to the wants of the family and without any regard to symmetry or convenience. It was absolutely impossible for Napoleon and his suite to find lodging there, enlargements were indispensable, and Napoleon remained at The Briers while they were made.

26. "The Code Napoleon, that elaborate system of jurisprudence in the formation of which the Emperor laboured personally along with the most eminent lawyers and enlightened men of the time, was a boon of inestimable value to France. It was the first uniform system of laws which the French monarchy had ever possessed; and being drawn up with consummate skill and wisdom, it at this day forms the code not only of France but of a great portion of Europe besides. Justice as between man and man was administered on sound

and fixed principles, and by unimpeached tribunals. The arbitrary commission courts of Napoleon interfered with nothing but offences real or alleged against the authority of the Emperor.

"The clergy were appointed universally under the direction of government; they were also its direct stipendiaries; hence nothing could be more complete than their subjection to its pleasure. Education became a part of the regular business of the state; all the schools and colleges being placed under the immediate care of one of Napoleon's ministers, all prizes and bursaries bestowed by the government, and the whole system so arranged that it was hardly possible for any youth who exhibited remarkable talents to avoid the temptations to a military career which on every side surrounded him. The chief distinctions and emoluments were everywhere reserved for those who excelled in accomplishments likely to be serviceable in war; and the *Lyceums,* or schools, set expressly apart for military students, were invested with numberless attractions, scarcely to be resisted by a young imagination. The army, as it was the sole basis of Napoleon's power, was also at all times the primary object of his thoughts. Every institution of the state was subservient and ministered to it, and none more efficaciously than the imperial system of education.

"The ranks of the army, however, were filled during the whole reign of Napoleon by *compulsion.* The conscription-law of 1798 acquired under him the character of a settled and regular part of the national system; and its oppressive influence was such as never before exhausted, through a long term of years the best energies of a great and civilized people. Every male in France under the age of twenty-five was liable to be called on to serve in the ranks; and the regulations as to the procuring of substitutes were so narrow that young men of the best families were forced to comply in their own persons with the stern requisition. The first conscription-list for the year included all under the age of twenty; and the results of the ballot within this class amounted to nearly 80,000 names. These were first called on, but if the service of the Emperor demanded further supply, the lists of those aged twenty-two, twenty-three, twenty-four, and twenty-five, were successively resorted to. There was no exemption for any one who seemed able to bear arms. The only child of his parents, the young husband and father were forced, like any others, to abandon fireside, profession, all the ties and hopes of life on a moment's notice; and there is nothing in the history of modern Europe so remarkable as that the French people should have submitted during sixteen years to the constant operation of a despotic law, which thus sapped all the foundations of social happiness, and condemned the rising hopes of the nation to bleed and die by millions in distant wars, undertaken solely for the gratification of one man's insatiable ambition."—*History of Napoleon Buonaparte.*

27. Talleyrand, and others only second to him in influence, were in communication with the Bourbons before the allies crossed the Rhine.

28. Napoleon had such an unconquerable aversion to Sir H. Lowe, whom he only saw three times, that he said only a short time before he died:—" I am going to die and escape from my gaoler, and I hope if God damns me, he will not give me another Hudson Lowe for my devil."

"I have seen Napoleon at his toilet. When he dresses himself, he is assisted by Marchand, St. Denis, and Novarre. One of the latter holds a glass before him, and the other the necessary shaving implements, whilst Marchand is ready to hand him his clothes, his eau-de-Cologne, &c. When he has shaved one side of his face, he says to Novarre, 'Is it done?' After the reply, he turns to the other side. When he has finished they hold the glass in front of him, and he examines to see if he is perfectly clean-shaven. If he sees or feels that any still remains, he sometimes takes one of them by the ear, or gives him a slight pat on the cheek, saying in a cheerful voice, 'Ah, miscreant! why did you say it was done?' This is probably what has given rise to the statement that he beat and maltreated his servants. He then washes his face with eau-de-Cologne and water, sprinkles some eau-de-Cologne over himself, carefully cleans his teeth, often has his body rubbed with a flesh-brush, changes his linen and flannel shirt. He then puts on a pair of brown nankeen breeches, a white waistcoat, silk stockings, shoes with gold buckles, a green coat with a single row of white buttons, a black cravat, and a small black three-cornered hat with a tricoloured cockade. When he is not in undress he always wears the grand cross of the legion of honour. When he has put on his coat, Marchand hands him a little bonbonnière, his snuff-box, his handkerchief scented with eau-de-Cologne, and he leaves the room."—*Napoléon dans l'Exil.*

29. On board the *Bellerophon* Bonaparte admitted that the Duke of Wellington, equal to himself in all other military qualities, was superior in prudence.

30. The position of the Duke of Wellington was before the village of Mont St. Jean, about a mile and a half in advance of the small town of Waterloo, on a rising ground, having a gentle and regular declivity before it; beyond this a plain of about a mile in breadth; and then the opposite heights of La Belle Alliance, on which the enemy would of course form their line. The Duke had now with him about 75,000 men in all; of whom about 30,000 were English. He formed his first line of the troops on which he could most surely rely—the greater part of the British foot—the men of Brunswick and Nassau, and three corps of Hanoverians and Belgians. Behind this the ground sinks and rises again. The second line, formed in rear of the first, was composed of the troops whose spirit and discipline were more doubtful, or who had suffered most in the action of Quatre Bras; and behind them all lay the horse. Napoleon had in the field 75,000 men, all French veterans, each of whom was in his own estimation worth one Englishman, and two Prussians, Dutch, or Belgians. Wellington's men, however, had had some hours of repose, whereas the army of Napoleon had been on the march all through the hours of tempestuous darkness, and the greater part of them reached not the heights of Belle Alliance until the morning of the 18th was considerably advanced. Napoleon had feared nothing so much as that Wellington would continue his retreat on Brussels and Antwerp, thus deferring the great battle until the Russians should approach the valley of the Rhine; and when on reaching the eminence of La Belle Alliance, he beheld the army drawn up on the opposite side, his joy was great. "At last, then," he exclaimed, "at last, then, I have these English in my grasp."

31. Sir John Moore thought very differently of the English soldiers, and he must be allowed to have known them more familiarly than even the great genius who so arbitrarily condemns them. Thus of his celebrated retreat Napier (*History of the War of the Peninsula*) well says,—" Moore felt that, in doing so, he compromised the safety of his own army, that he must glide along the edge of a precipice; that he must cross a gulf on a rotten plank; *but he also knew the martial qualities of his soldiers;* he had confidence in his own genius, and the occasion being worthy of a great deed, he dared essay it, *even against Napoleon.*" Further, after incessant fighting against a force six times as large, after typhus and other diseases given from the Spaniards who crossed the English line of retreat in a disorganized mass our men were not so demoralized but they could fight. "It is well said," says Napier, "that a British army may be gleaned in a retreat, but cannot be reaped; whatever may be their misery, the soldiers will always be found clean at review, ready at a fight; and scarcely was this order issued, when the line of battle, so attenuated before, was filled with vigorous men, full of confidence and valour."— How these behaved we know.

32. Josephine's letter to Napoleon on the birth of the King of Rome:

"Navarre.

"SIRE,—Amidst the numerous congratulations which you receive from all parts of Europe, from every town in France, and every regiment of the army, can the feeble voice of a woman reach you? And will you condescend to listen to her who so often consoled you in your sorrows, and assuaged the pangs of your heart, when she speaks only of the happiness which has just crowned your wishes? Being no longer your wife, dare I offer my congratulations on your becoming a father? Yes, doubtless, sire! for my soul renders the same justice to yours as yours to mine. I conceive what you now experience as readily as you divine my emotions on this occasion; though separated, we are united by the sympathy which bids defiance to events.

"I should have been glad to learn the birth of the King of Rome from yourself, and not by the Canon of Evreux, or the

Prefect's courier; but I am well aware that your first attentions are due to the members of the Corps Diplomatique, to your family, and above all, to the happy Princess who has just realized your dearest hopes. She cannot be more tenderly devoted to you than I am; but she has had it in her power to do more for your happiness by assuring the welfare of France; she has therefore a right to your first sentiments, to all your cares; and I, who was your companion in misfortune only, can claim but a far inferior place to that which Maria Louisa occupies in your affection. You will have watched round her bed, and embraced your son, before you take up your pen to converse with your best friend. I will wait!

"It is however impossible for me to defer telling you that, more than any one on earth, I share in your joy. You will not doubt my sincerity when I say that, far from being afflicted with a sacrifice so necessary to the repose of all, I rejoice that it has been made, *now that I suffer alone. Suffer,* do I say? No! since *you* are contented; and my only regret is, that I have not yet done sufficient to prove how dear you were to me!"— *Mémoires de Josephine.*

33. Captain Basil Hall thus describes Napoleon at Longwood (1817): "Bonaparte struck me as differing considerably from all the pictures and busts I had seen of him. His face and figure looked much broader and more square—larger, indeed, in every way than any representation I had met with. His corpulency, at this time reported to be excessive, was by no means remarkable. His flesh looked, on the contrary, firm and muscular. There was not the least trace of colour in his cheeks; in fact, his skin was more like marble than ordinary flesh. Not the smallest wrinkle was discernible on his brow, nor an approach to a furrow on any part of his countenance. His health and spirits, judging from appearances, were excellent; though at this period it was generally believed in England that he was fast sinking under a complication of diseases, and that his spirits were entirely gone. His manner of speaking was rather slow than otherwise, and perfectly distinct; and he waited with great patience and kindness for my answers to his questions. The brilliant and sometimes dazzling expression of eye could not be overlooked. It was not,

however, a permanent lustre, for it was only remarkable when he was excited by some point of particular interest. It is impossible to imagine an expression of more entire mildness, I may almost call it of benignity and kindliness, than that which played over his features during the whole interview. If, therefore, he was at this time out of health and in low spirits, his power of self-command must have been even more extraordinary than is generally supposed; for his whole deportment, his conversation, and the expression of his face, indicated a frame in perfect health, and a mind at ease."

Byron says of him at this period:—

> "Well thy soul hath brook'd the morning tide,
> With that innate untaught philosophy,
> Which be it wisdom, coldness, or deep pride,
> Is gall and wormwood to an enemy.
> When the whole host of hatred stood hard by,
> To watch and mock thee shrinking, thou hast smiled
> With a sedate and all-enduring eye;
> When fortune fled her spoiled and favourite child,
> He stood unbow'd beneath the ills upon him piled.
> * * * * *
> Conqueror and captive of the earth art thou.
> She trembles at thee still—and thy wild name
> Was ne'er more bruited in men's minds than now
> That thou art nothing, save the jest of Fame
> Who woo'd thee once thy vassal, and became
> The flatterer of thy fierceness, till thou wert
> A god unto thyself, nor less the same
> To the astounded kingdoms all inert
> Who deem'd thee for a time whate'er
> Thou didst assert."

34. Of Napoleon, Duroc said to Caulaincourt, "The Emperor, my dear Caulaincourt, appears to me to be endowed with a variety of mental faculties, any one of which would suffice to distinguish a man from the multitude. For example, he is the greatest captain of the age — a sovereign whose ministers are merely his clerks — a statesman who directs the whole business of the country, and superintends every branch of the service; and yet this Colossus of gigantic proportions can descend with wonderful facility to the most trivial details of private life. He can regulate the expenditure of his household as he regulates the finances of the empire."—*Recollections of Caulaincourt.*

35. "In conversation on general topics, Napoleon's interlocutor would find himself perfectly at his ease, and Napoleon maintained his share in the discussion with a grace and *bonhommie* which never failed to exercise a captivating influence. But in a conversation on any important subject, the Emperor was cautious and reserved; he was always master of himself, and he imposed a certain degree of restraint on the person with whom he was discoursing. He seemed, as it were, to take advantage of his exalted position, and willingly or reluctantly, his interlocutor was almost always brought over to his way of thinking."—*Recollections of Caulaincourt.*

36. "In his social relations, Bonaparte's temper was bad; but his fits of ill-humour passed away like a cloud, and spent themselves in words. His violent language and bitter imprecations were frequently premeditated. When he was going to reprimand any one, he liked to have a witness present.

"He possessed every requisite for being what is called in society an agreeable man, except the will to be so. His manner was imposing rather than pleasing, and those who did not know him well experienced in his presence an involuntary feeling of awe. In the drawing-room where Josephine did the honours, with so much grace and affability, all was gaiety and ease, and no one felt the presence of a superior; but on Bonaparte's entrance all was changed, and every eye was directed towards him, to read his humour in his countenance, whether he intended to be silent or talkative, dull or cheerful.

"When in good humour his usual tokens of kindness consisted in a little rap on the head, or a slight pinch of the ear. In his most friendly conversations with those whom he admitted into his intimacy he would say, 'You are a fool,' 'a simpleton,' 'a ninny,' 'a blockhead.' These, and a few other words of like import, enabled him to vary his catalogue of compliments; but he never employed them angrily, and the tone in which they were uttered sufficiently indicated that they were meant in kindness.

"Bonaparte had many singular habits and tastes. Whenever he experienced any vexation, or when any unpleasant thought occupied his mind, he would hum something which was far from resembling a tune, for his voice was very unmusical. He would at the same time seat himself before the writing-table and swing back in his chair so far that I have often been fearful of his falling. He would vent his ill-humour on the right arm of his chair, mutilating it with his pen-knife, which he seemed to keep for no other purpose.

"Bonaparte was insensible to the charms of poetic harmony. He had not even sufficient ear to feel the rhythm of poetry, and he never could recite a verse without violating the metre; yet the grand ideas of poetry charmed him.

"Gallantry to women was by no means a trait in Napoleon's character. He seldom said anything agreeable to them, and frequently addressed to them the rudest and most extraordinary remarks. To one he would say, 'Heavens, how red your elbows are!' to another, 'What an ugly head-dress you have got!' and to a third, 'Your dress is none of the cleanest . . . . Do you never change your gown? I have seen you in that twenty times.'"

"Amongst Bonaparte's singular habits was that of seating himself on any table which happened to be of a suitable height for him. He would often sit on mine, resting his left arm on my right shoulder, and swinging his left leg, which did not reach the ground; and while he dictated to me he would jolt the table so that I could scarcely write.

"Bonaparte was neither malignant nor vindictive. I cannot certainly defend him against all the reproaches which he incurred through the imperious law of war and cruel necessity; but I may say that he has often been unjustly accused. None but those who are blinded by fury will call him a Nero or a Caligula. I think I have avowed his faults with sufficient candour to entitle me to credit when I speak in his commendation, and I declare that out of the field of battle Bonaparte had a kind and feeling heart. He was very fond of children, a trait which seldom distinguishes a bad man. In the relations of private life, to call him amiable would not be using too strong a word, and he was very indulgent to the weakness of human nature. The contrary opinion is too firmly fixed in some minds for me to hope to root it out. I shall, I fear, have contradictors, but I address myself to those who look for truth. To judge impartially we must take into account the influence which time and circumstance exercise on men; and distinguish between the different characters of the collegian, the general, the consul, and the emperor."—*Bourrienne's Memoirs of Napoleon.*

37. Napoleon was as essentially and irreclaimably a despot as warrior; but his successor, whether a Bourbon or a Bonaparte, was likely to be a constitutional sovereign. The tyranny of a meaner hand would not have been endured after that precedent. Napoleon broke down the barriers everywhere of custom and prejudice; and revolutionized the spirit of the Continent. His successes and his double downfall taught absolute princes their weakness, and injured nations their strength.

38. Napoleon eat and slept according to the time, circumstances and situation in which he found himself; his slumber was ordinarily sweet and tranquil; if grief or any incident interrupted it, he jumped out of bed, called for a light, walked, worked, fixed his mind upon an object, sometimes he remained in the dark, changed his room, got into another bed, or stretched himself on a sofa. He was up at two, three, four o'clock in the morning. He called some one to keep him company, to discourse upon recollections, or passing events, while they awaited the daylight. He went out as soon as it appeared, he took a turn, and when the sun showed himself, he went in and went to bed again where he remained a long time, or a short, according to the appearance of the day. If it was unpleasant and he felt irritated and uneasy, he had recourse to the method before explained, he changed from bed to sofa, and from sofa to bed; variety did him good. "Doctors," said he to Antommarchi, "have the ordering of the table; it is but fair that I give you a description of mine; this is how it is arranged, one dish of soup, two of meat, one of vegetables, a salad when I can have it, compose the whole. I take half a bottle of claret much diluted, and a little pure at the end of dinner. For the rest I eat quickly and masticate little, for my meals do not take much of my time. You do not approve of that, but in my situation what is the advantage of mastication?"

39. Of all the popular engines which moved the spleen of Napoleon, the most offensive was a newspaper (*L'Ambigu*) published in the French language in London, by one Peltier, a

royalist emigrant; and in spite of all the advice which could be offered, he at length condescended to prosecute the author in the English courts of law. M. Peltier had the good fortune to retain as his counsel Mr. Mackintosh (afterwards Sir James) an advocate of most brilliant talents, and moreover especially distinguished for his support of the original principles of the French revolution. On the trial which ensued, this orator, in defence of his client, delivered a philippic against the personal character and ambitious measures of Napoleon, immeasurably more calculated to injure the Chief Consul in public opinion throughout Europe, than all the efforts of a thousand newspapers; and though the jury found Peltier guilty of libel, the result was on the whole a signal triumph to the party of which he had been the organ.

40. Bonaparte held the liberty of the press in the greatest horror; and so violent was his passion, when anything was urged in its favour, that he seemed to labour under a nervous attack. Great man as he was, he was sorely afraid of little paragraphs.—*Bourrienne's Memoirs.*

41. Bonaparte did not study much; he read all the newspapers that were brought to him, with attention. But during whole hours he was occupied in turning over page after page of *Chambaud's Dictionary.* There is some amusement to be found in Johnson's Dictionary, on account of the choice quotations it contains, but there is nothing of the kind in Chambaud. I suppose he kept his eyes mechanically fixed upon the book as an excuse for thinking.—*Relation written at St. Helena of the Last Six Weeks of the Emperor Napoleon's Life, by John Monkhouse, a naval officer.*

42. Fouché furnishes us with an amusing proof how Napoleon himself was subjected to a system of espionage:

"One day Bonaparte observed, that considering my acknowledged ability, he was astonished I did not perform my functions better—that there were several things of which I was ignorant. 'Yes,' replied I, 'there certainly are things of which I *was* ignorant, but which I now know well enough. For instance, a little man muffled up in a grey cloak, and accompanied by a single servant, often steals out on a dark evening from the Tuileries, enters a closed carriage, and drives off to Signora

G——. This little man is yourself; and yet this fanciful songstress jilts you continually, out of love for Rode the fiddler.' The Consul answered not a word: he turned his back, rung, and I immediately withdrew."—*Fouché's Memoires*, tom. i. p. 233.

Fouché was perhaps the firmest support of despotism in France. He did not scruple to fulfil the most tyrannical wishes of the Emperor; still less to approve his most tyrannical pretensions. He was more crafty than Napoleon himself, and as supple as crafty.

"This is the way your majesty should always govern," he said. "The legislative body arrogates to itself the right of representing the nation in place of the sovereign! Dissolve any body, sire, that thus dares to interfere with your royal prerogative. Had Louis XVI. done so, he would be living and reigning this very day." The Emperor stared: "How is this, Duke of Otranto? Are you not one of those who sent Louis to the scaffold?" "Yes, sire; and that is the first service I had the honour of rendering your majesty."—*Court and Camp of Bonaparte.*

43. "Bonaparte," said Mr. Wyndham in Parliament (1803), "is the Hannibal who has sworn to devote his life to the destruction of England. War cannot be far off, and I believe it would be much safer to anticipate the blow than to expect it. I would advise ministers to appeal to the high-minded and proud of heart; whether they succeed or not, we shall not then go down like the *Augustuli*." "The destruction of this country," said Mr. Sheridan, "is the first vision that breaks on the French Consul through the gleam of the morning; this is his last prayer at night, to whatever deity he may address it, whether to Jupiter or to Mahomet, to the goddess of battles, or the goddess of reason. Look at the map of Europe, from which France was said to be expunged, and now see nothing but France. If the ambition of Bonaparte be immeasurable, there are abundant reasons why it should be progressive."

Napoleon's Funeral at St. Helena.—Napoleon was buried on the 8th of May. All the inhabitants were assembled at Longwood to pay their last token of respect to the remains of the captive who had rendered their island immortal. At half-past twelve o'clock at noon, the grenadiers placed the heavy triple coffin of tin, lead, and mahogany upon the hearse. It was drawn by four horses. Twelve grenadiers walked by the side of the coffin to take it upon their shoulders where the bad state of the road prevented the horses from advancing. The Emperor's household, dressed in deepest mourning, immediately followed the hearse. Their hearts were stricken with grief, deep and unaffected. The admiral and the governor, with the officers of the staff, respectfully joined the procession on horseback. All the inhabitants of St. Helena, men, women, and children, in a long winding train, reverently followed. The English garrison which had been stationed on the island to guard the Emperor, two thousand five hundred strong, lined the whole of the left side of the road nearly to the grave. Bands of music, stationed at intervals, breathed their requiems upon the still air. The soldiers, as the procession passed, fell into the line and followed to the grave.

At length the hearse stopped. The grenadiers took the coffin on their shoulders, and carried it along a narrow path, which had been constructed on the side of the mountain, to the lonely place of burial. The coffin was placed on the verge of the grave. The Abbé Vignali recited the burial service, while all were overpowered by the unwonted solemnity and sublimity of the scene. During the funeral-march, the admiral's ship in the harbour had fired minute-guns; and as the coffin descended to its chamber of massive masonry, deep in the earth, three successive volleys from a battery of fifteen guns, discharged over the grave, reverberated along the cliffs and crags of St. Helena. The willows which overhung the tomb were immediately stripped of their foliage, as each one wished to carry away some souvenir of the most extraordinary man the world has ever known. The officers of the household of the Emperor upon the day of his death, had ordered a stone to be prepared to rest upon his grave with this simple inscription:—

NAPOLEON,

BORN AT AJACCIO THE 15TH OF AUGUST, 1769,
DIED AT ST. HELENA THE 5TH OF MAY, 1821.

The graver had already cut this inscription, when Sir Hudson Lowe informed the friends of the Emperor, that the orders of the British government were imperative that no inscription could be allowed on the tomb, but simply the words, General Bonaparte.—*Abbott's Life of Nap. Bonaparte.*

45. *Napoleon's Remains at Paris.* The whole National Guard of Paris was drawn out to escort the remains of Napoleon. The Polish emigrants, many of them men of high distinction, sent a deputation earnestly requesting permission to assist in the funeral ceremonies of the only monarch who had ever expressed any sympathy in their cause. Louis Philippe, the king of the French, with all the members of the royal family, and the members of the chamber of deputies, and the chamber of peers, were assembled beneath the gorgeous dome of the Invalides, to render homage to the returning Emperor. The embellishments in Paris along the path of the procession, surpassed everything which had ever been attempted before. The arch of triumph was decorated with most imposing grandeur. A colossal image of the Emperor stood upon its towering summit, looking serenely down upon his own marvellous triumph, and surrounded by those flags and eagles which his victories had rendered immortal.

The view down the spacious avenue of the Champs Elysées, was imposing in the extreme. Each side was lined with lofty columns, surmounted by gilt eagles, and decorated with tri-coloured flags. Colossal statues, triumphal arches, immense vases blazing with variegated flames, and the assemblage of a countless multitude of spectators, presented a spectacle never to be forgotten.

The imperial car was composed of five distinct parts, the basement, the pedestal, the caryatides, the shield, and the cenotaph. The basement rested on four massive gilt wheels. This basement, which was twenty-five feet long, and six feet high, and all the rich ornaments with which it was profusely embellished, were covered with frosted gold. Upon this basement stood groups of cherubs, seven feet high, supporting a pedestal eighteen feet long, covered with burnished gold. This pedestal, elevated thirteen feet from the ground, was constructed with a heavy cornice richly ornamented. It was hung in purple velvet, falling in graceful drapery to the ground, embroidered with gold and spotted with bees. Upon this elevated pedestal stood fourteen caryatides, antique figures larger than life, and entirely covered with gold, supporting with their heads and hands an immense shield of solid gold. This shield was of oval form, and eighteen feet in length, and richly decorated with all appropriate ornaments. Upon the top of this shield nearly fifty feet from the ground, was placed the cenotaph, an exact copy of Napoleon's coffin. It was slightly veiled with purple crape, embroidered with golden bees. On the cenotaphs upon a velvet cushion were placed the sceptre, the sword of justice, the imperial crown in gold, and embellished with precious stones. Such is a general description of this funeral-car, the most sumptuous that was probably ever constructed.

The chariot was drawn by sixteen black horses, yoked four abreast. These steeds were so entirely caparisoned in cloth of gold, that their feet only could be seen. Waving plumes of white feathers adorned their heads and manes. Sixteen grooms wearing the imperial livery led the horses.

At half-past nine in the morning, after prayers had been read over the body, twenty-four seamen raised the coffin on their shoulders, and following the procession of the clergy, conveyed it to the Grecian Temple. There it was deposited for a short time while the clergy again chanted prayers. The seamen then again took up their precious load, and conveyed it to the triumphal car. It was placed in the interior of the vehicle, its apparent place being occupied by the cenotaph on the summit of the shield. As the car commenced its solemn movement, the sun and moon were both shining in the serene and cloudless sky, gilding with extraordinary splendour this unparalleled scene. No language can describe the enthusiasm inspired as the car passed slowly along, surrounded by the five hundred sailors who had accompanied the remains from St. Helena, and preceded and followed by the most imposing military array which the kingdom of France could furnish. More than a million of people were assembled along the line of march to welcome back the Emperor. All the bells in Paris were tolling. Music from innumerable bands filled the air, blending with the solemn peal of minute-guns and of salutes of honour from many batteries. The multitude shouted, and sung, and wept. In a roar as of thunder, the Marseillese Hymn resounded from ten thousand voices, and was echoed and re-echoed along the interminable lines.

The Church of the Invalides in the splendour of its adornings resembled a fairy palace. The walls were elegantly hung with rich drapery of violet velvet, studded with stars of gold, and bordered with a massive gold fringe. The eight columns which supported the dome were entirely covered with velvet, studded with golden bees. It would require a volume to describe the splendours of this room. Beneath its lofty dome, where the massive tomb of Napoleon was ulteriorly to be erected, a tomb which would cost millions of money, and which would require the labour of years, a magnificent cenotaph, in the form of a temple superbly gilded, was reared. This temple was pronounced by all judges to be one of the happiest efforts of decorative art. Here the remains of the Emperor were for a time to repose. Thirty-six thousand spectators were seated upon immense platforms, on the esplanade of the Invalides. Six thousand spectators thronged the seats of the spacious portico. In the interior of the church were assembled, the clergy, the members of the two chambers of deputies and of peers, and all the members of the royal family, and others of the most distinguished personages of France and of Europe. As the coffin, preceded by the Prince de Joinville was borne along the nave upon the shoulders of thirty-two of Napoleon's old guard, all rose and bowed in homage to the mighty dead. Louis Philippe, surrounded by the great officers of state, then stepped forward to receive the remains. "Sire," said the prince, "I present to you the body of the Emperor Napoleon." "I receive it," replied the king, "in the name of France." Then taking from the hand of Marshal Soult the sword of Napoleon, and presenting it to General Bertrand, he said "General, I charge you to place this glorious sword of the Emperor upon this coffin." The king then returned to his throne, the coffin was placed in the catafalque, and the last wish of Napoleon was gratified. The funeral mass was then celebrated. The king of France sat upon one side of the altar accompanied by the queen, and all the princes and princesses of the royal family. The ministers and the marshals of the kingdom, the archbishop of Paris with his assistant bishops and clergy, and all the prominent civil and military authorities of France, gathered reverentially around the mausoleum in this last sublime act of a nation's love and gratitude. As the solemn strains of Mozart's Requiem, performed by three hundred musicians floated through the air, all hearts were intensely moved. Thus ended a ceremony which in all the elements of moral sublimity has no parallel.—*Abbott's Life of Napoleon Bonaparte.*

46. *Napoleon's Height, &c.* The entire height of the body from the top of the head to the heels was five feet two inches and four lines, equal to five feet six inches, and twenty-two forty-fifths of an inch, the French foot being greater than the English in the proportion of sixteen to fifteen.

The extent from the extremity of the middle finger of one hand to that of the other, was five feet two inches.

The length from the top of the head to the chin was seven inches and six lines.

The circumference of the head was twenty inches and ten lines. The forehead was high, the temples slightly depressed, the sinciput wide and very strongly defined.

I felt a curiosity to examine the head of this great man according to the craniological system of Drs. Gall and Spurzheim, the following are the signs which were most apparent on it: 1. Organ of dissimulation. 2. Organ of conquests. 3. Organ of kindness and benevolence. 4. Organ of imagination. 5. Organ of ambition and love of glory. Of intellectual faculties I found: 1. Organ of individuality. 2. Organ of locality, the relation of space. 3. Organ of calculation. 4. Organ of comparison. 5. Organ of causality, of the faculty of induction, of a philosophical head.—*Antommarchi's Last Days of Napoleon,* vol. 2, pp. 163-5.

INDEX.

	Page
ABDICATION	45
Acknowledgment of the title of Emperor	26
After Wagram	33
After Waterloo	53
Affection of strangers	76
Alteration of the abdication	46
An American on Napoleon at Helena	50
An open enemy	37
Answer to a deputation	25
Aristocracy	81
Arrangement of ideas	10
A soldier's duty	6
A taste for founding	11
At Lodi	165
Attachment	127
Austria and the French Republic	12
Austria declares war	41
Austrians at Marengo	68
APHORISMS	146 to 152
Battle at Montereau	44
Beautiful Italy	131
Before departing for Elba	48
Bernadotte	34, 110
Bessière's tomb	40

INDEX.

	Page
Bidding adieu to troops	13
Blucher	103
Bonaparte's assistant consuls	155
Bonaparte's temper and tastes	174
Bonaparte and the liberty of the press	177
Bridge of Lodi	10
British magnanimity	123
Bust of Napoleon's son	101
Cannon ball at Friedland	30
Cardinal Fesch and the Russian war	163
Cerachi and the fanatic of Schœnbrunn	96
Character of Duroc	68
Christianity	20
Christianity and Mahomet	18
Cipriani	88
Climate of France	123
Codicil to Napoleon's will	129
Conduct of English sailors	59
Confession to Caulaincourt	46
Confidence in doctors	106
Confirmation	2
Conscription	67
Conversations with ladies	99
Constantinople	74
Contagion of crime	100
Contentions at Longwood	74
Conversation	174
Cornwallis	106
Counsel to his son	132
Day and night work	15
Death	144
Death of Desaix	22
Description of Napoleon at Longwood	172
Devotion of the soldiers	19
Directions to O'Meara	110
Directors	16

INDEX.

	Page
Duroc	40
Duroc's opinion of Napoleon	173
Early youth	65
Effeminate men	6
Egypt and fate	17
England and liberty	79
English soldiers	103
Europe	7
Farewell to France	61
Fate versus medicine	77
Ferdinand of Spain	129
First introduction to Sir Hudson Lowe	84
Flogging in the army	61
Frederic the Great's sword	28
French and English eaters	103
Friendship	20
From Elba	49
Gaming	63
General Bertrand's children	125
General Clarke	11
General Dejean	100
Giacominetta	122
Gift to Captain Poppleton	143
Goethe and the German drama	31
Good mothers	24
Head and tongue	22
Heroic times	32
Histories of France	68
Idea of the desert	19
If	82
If St. Helena were France	125
Impossible	9
Imprisonment at St. Helena	60

INDEX.

	Page
Intended suicide at Fontainebleau	47
Ivan Petrowisk	36
Jesus Christ	78
Joseph Bonaparte	102
Josephine	153
Josephine's letter to a friend before marriage	154
Josephine's extravagance	154
Josephine on the birth of the King of Rome	170
L'Ambigu	176
La Nouvelle Heloise	72
Lannes	81
Lannes at Lodi	64
Last interview with the governor	87
Last meeting with Josephine	44
Last words	145
Legitimacy	126
Letter to Las Cases	92
List of books for a camp library	157
Longwood	167
Lord Whitworth and the peace of Amiens	42
Loss of the "Italy"	19
Losses during the Russian war	163
Louis Bonaparte	83
Love and glory	13
Mamma Letitia	127
Man an animal	95
Man's ingratitude	48
Marie Louise	38, 71
Marriage of Marie Louise	107
Marshal Bessières	38
Marshal Turenne	8
Medicine	132
Medicines	76
Men	108
Men and women in sickness	125

INDEX.

	Page
Men in Italy	7
Men often children	71
Message to the governor	98
Miserable man	76
Mlle. de Colombier	3
Mme. de Maintenon and Mme. de Sévigné	75
Mme. de Staël	80
Monk and Napoleon politically compared	143
Montchenu	87
Montholon	84
Mr. Wyndham on Bonaparte	178
Murat	22
Murat's desertion	37
Music	132
Myself	61
Napoleon's German master	1
Napoleon states his opinions	3
Napoleon before the Convention	6
Napoleon Commander-in-chief	8
Napoleon and the dragoon	10
Napoleon and Mme. de Staël	11
Napoleon upon the King's death	15
Napoleon and Bourrienne	15
Napoleon's bulletins	20
Napoleon's religion	23
Napoleon and the young English sailor	25
Napoleon and the other European sovereigns	26
Napoleon and the peasant woman	27
Napoleon on literature	29
Napoleon's soldiers	30
Napoleon's 38th birthday	30
Napoleon and Josephine at Etampes	32
Napoleon on Moscow	36
Napoleon at Dresden	43
Napoleon at Malmaison	55
Napoleon and the village child	57
Napoleon's son and France	58

Napoleon a fatalist	62
Napoleon's handwriting	64
Napoleon and the Jews	77
Napoleon's family	79
Napoleon's divorce	82
Napoleon's domestics	85
Napoleon's dislike	86
Napoleon out of humour	86
Napoleon's name	87
Napoleon on Waterloo	88
Napoleon's mother	98
Napoleon happy	100
Napoleon sensitive of intrusion	111
Napoleon's father	124
Napoleon's ornaments	124
Napoleon's France	127
Napoleon and the British	141
Napoleon's birth	153
Napoleon's hats and boots	157
Napoleon and the Koran	158
Napoleon on Murat	161
Napoleon's constancy	162
Napoleon at Dresden	164
Napoleon at Court	164
Napoleon and the English government	164
Napoleon's aversion to Sir Hudson Lowe	169
Napoleon's toilet	169
Napoleon a despot	176
Napoleon's diet and sleep	176
Napoleon and Chambaud's Dictionary	177
Napoleon watched	177
Napoleon's funeral at St. Helena	178
Napoleon's remains at Paris	180
Napoleon's height, &c.	183
Naples	144
Occupation	60
On the invasion of England	69

INDEX.

	Page
Organized matter	101
Paoli	2
Paris in 1814	44
Paris	81
Patron saints	104
Pavia and plunder	10
Picture of St. Jerome	9
Polignac's wife	26
Poniatowski	43
Poor France	67
Pope's Iliad	142
Predestinarianism	62
Preference for monarchy	4
Prince Charles	19
Proclamation before starting for England	16
Proclamation before disembarking	17
Proclamation to the French	58
Proposition to make Napoleon Grand Elector	22
Proposed surrender of Illyria, &c.	83
Protest from the Bellerophon	60
Provinces and hearts	13
Quarters of an hour	123
Reasons for hostility to Roman Catholicism	23
Regrets	142
Religion and the French	24
Remarks on Sir H. Lowe's letters	102
Renown	78
Report of death and its result	35
Required surrender of the crown	44
Restoration of the Bourbons	45
Respect the burden	75
Rest	128
Rewards	24
Rousseau	21
Roveredo	166

INDEX.

	Page
Savary's system of espionage	156
School fête	2
School life	153
Second interview with Sir H. Lowe	85
Sir Thomas Strange	98
Sir John Moore	171
Soult at Eylau	162
Starting for Erfurt	38
St. Simon's daughter	31
St. Helena	69
St. Helena and Elba compared	69
Study	5
Suicide from disappointed love	27
Suicide	47
Survey of the English coast	15
Swiss enthusiasm	13
Talleyrand	75
Talleyrand and the Bourbons	169
Temper in women	71
Tents	64
The art of healing	129
The barber's wife	3
The Bourbons and the mob	20
The capital of Russia	59
The Code Napoleon	73, 167
The crowd around the Champs Elysées	57
The crown in the mire	22
The dilatory orderly-officer	28
The Dresden magistrates	39
The Duke of Wellington	101, 170
The Duke of Wellington's position at Waterloo	170
The dying Prussian	39
The Elysian fields	143
The Emperor Alexander and Turkey	80
The Emperor Francis visits Napoleon	28
The English government and nation	58
The fate of war	43

INDEX.

	Page
The First Consul and the mails	155
The fishwoman disconcerted	6
The greater number	21
The Italians	130
The King of Rome at Compiègne	34
The "man of destiny"	164
The new constitution	5
The passage of the Niemen	163
The pomp of the throne	49
The priests	129
The Pyramids	18
The Saviour	112
The *savans* and the *demi-savans*	158
The school-girl of Ecouen	31
The sick and wounded	35
The sleeping sentinel	7
The Soul and the Scalpel	126
The state was myself	43
The "Times"	91
The trappings of royalty	26
The two Empresses	72
The wounded	23
The 20th June, 1792	4
Theophilanthropists	14
Time	16
Title of nobility	9
To Josephine	33
To Murat	37
To the officers of state	33
To the soldiers before Moscow	34
Toulon	5
Tragedy	69
Treaty of Campo Formio	14
Treaties with England	23
Troy and Moscow	35
Try	40
Two paths	40
Tyrant's skin	77

INDEX.

	Page
Valour	38
Veteran advice	8
Victory	19, 29, 64
War	30
War and ambition	40
War to the death	37
Weakness overbearing	78
What is life worth?	13
What is popularity?	65

CHISWICK PRESS:—PRINTED BY WHITTINGHAM AND WILKINS,
TOOKS COURT, CHANCERY LANE.

A List of Books

PUBLISHING BY

SAMPSON LOW, SON, AND MARSTON,

Crown Buildings, 188, *Fleet Street*.

[*May*, 1868.

NEW ILLUSTRATED WORKS.

THE STORY WITHOUT AN END. From the German of Carové. By Sarah Austin. Illustrated with Sixteen Original Water-Colour Drawings by E. V. B., printed in Fac-simile and numerous Illustrations on wood. Small 4to. cloth extra, 12s.; or inlaid on side with floral ornament on ivory, 15s.; or in morocco, 21s.

*** Also a Large Paper Edition, with the Plates mounted (only 250 copies printed), morocco, ivory inlaid, 31s. 6d.

"*Nowhere will he find the Book of Nature more freshly and beautifully opened for him than in ' The Story without an End,' of its kind one of the best that was ever written.*"—Quarterly Review.

"*We have here a most beautiful edition of Mrs. Austin's well-known translation of 'The Story without an End,' illustrated by E. V. B. with even more than her accustomed poetical grace and fancy. It is difficult to select when all the illustrations are so delicately beautiful, but we cannot help pointing out several that strike us especially. . . . But it is quite impossible to describe these illustrations. We must refer our readers to the book itself if they wish to see a perfect development of the grace, fancy, and true poetical genius for which the pictures of E. V. B. have long been remarkable.*"—Spectator.

"*The illustrations are worthy of the text, for they are generally coloured in strict accordance with nature, and have been printed with marvellous skill. Indeed, we do not hesitate to say that the plates in this volume are the best specimens of colour-printing we have ever seen.*"— Illustrated Times.

Also, illustrated by the same Artist,

Child's Play. Printed in fac-simile from Water-Colour Drawings, 7s. 6d.
Tennyson's May Queen. Illustrated on Wood. Large Paper Edition, 7s. 6d.

CHRISTIAN LYRICS. Chiefly selected from Modern Authors. 138 Poems, illustrated with upwards of 150 Engravings, under the superintendence of J. D. Cooper. Small 4to. cloth extra, 10s. 6d.; morocco, 21s.

The Poetry of Nature. Selected and Illustrated with Thirty-six Engravings by Harrison Weir. Crown 8vo. handsomely bound in cloth, gilt edges, 5s.; morocco, 10s. 6d.

*** Forming the new volume of Low's Choice Editions of Choice Books.

Choice Editions of Choice Books. New Editions. Illustrated by C. W. Cope, R.A., T. Creswick, R.A., Edward Duncan, Birket Foster, J. C. Horsley, A.R.A., George Hicks, R. Redgrave, R.A., C. Stonehouse, F. Tayler, George Thomas, H. J. Townshend, E. H. Wehnert, Harrison Weir, &c. Crown 8vo. cloth, 5s. each; mor. 10s. 6d.

Bloomfield's Farmer's Boy.	Keat's Eve of St. Agnes.
Campbell's Pleasures of Hope.	Milton's l'Allegro.
Cundall's Elizabethan Poetry.	Poetry of Nature.
Coleridge's Ancient Mariner.	Roger's Pleasures of Memory.
Goldsmith's Deserted Village.	Shakespeare's Songs and Sonnets.
Goldsmith's Vicar of Wakefield.	Tennyson's May Queen.
Gray's Elegy in a Churchyard.	Wordsworth's Pastoral Poems.

"*Such works are a glorious beatification for a poet. Such works as these educate townsmen, who, surrounded by dead and artificial things, as country people are by life and nature, scarcely learn to look at nature till taught by these concentrated specimens of her beauty.*"—Athenæum.

Bishop Heber's Hymns. An Illustrated Edition, with upwards of one hundred Designs. Engraved, in the first style of Art under the superintendence of J. D. Cooper. Small 4to. handsomely bound, price Half a Guinea; morocco, 21s.

The Divine and Moral Songs of Dr. Watts: a New and very choice Edition. Illustrated with One Hundred Woodcuts in the first style of the Art, from Original Designs by Eminent Artists; engraved by J. D. Cooper. Small 4to. cloth extra, price 7s. 6d.; morocco, 15s.

Artists and Arabs; or Sketching in Sunshine. By Henry Blackburn, author of "The Pyrenees," &c. Numerous Illustrations. Demy 8vo. cloth. 10s. 6d.

The Pyrenees; a Description of Summer Life at French Watering Places. By Henry Blackburn, author of "Travelling in Spain in the Present Day." With upwards of 100 Illustrations by Gustave Doré. Royal 8vo, cloth, 18s.; morocco, 25s.

Travelling in Spain in the present day by a party of Ladies and Gentlemen. By the same Author. With numerous Illustrations and Map of Route. Square 8vo. 16s.

Two Centuries of Song; or, Melodies, Madrigals, Sonnets, and other Occasional Verse of the English Poets of the last 200 years. With Critical and Biographical Notes by Walter Thornbury. Illustrated by Original Pictures of Eminent Artists. Drawn and Engraved especially for this work. Printed on toned paper, with coloured borders, designed by Henry Shaw, F.S.A. Very handsomely bound. Cloth extra, 21s.; morocco, 42s.

Milton's Paradise Lost. With the original Steel Engravings of John Martin. Printed on large paper, royal 4to. handsomely bound, 3*l*. 13*s*. 6*d*.; morocco extra, 5*l*. 15*s*. 6*d*.

Light after Darkness: Religious Poems by Harriet Beecher Stowe. With Illustrations. Small post 8vo. cloth, 3*s*. 6*d*.

Poems of the Inner Life. Selected chiefly from modern Authors, by permission. Small post 8vo. 6*s*.; gilt edges, 6*s*. 6*d*.

Favourite English Poems. *Complete Edition*. Comprising a Collection of the most celebrated Poems in the English Language, with but one or two exceptions unabridged, from Chaucer to Tennyson. With 300 Illustrations by the first Artists. Two vols. royal 8vo. half bound, top gilt, Roxburgh style, 1*l*. 18*s*.; antique calf, 3*l*. 3*s*.

⁎ Either Volume sold separately as distinct works. 1. " Early English Poems, Chaucer to Dyer." 2. " Favourite English Poems, Thomson to Tennyson." Each handsomely bound in cloth, 1*l*. 1*s*.

" One of the choicest gift-books of the year, " Favourite English Poems" is not a toy book, to be laid for a week on the Christmas table and then thrown aside with the sparkling trifles of the Christmas tree, but an honest book, to be admired in the season of pleasant remembrances for its artistic beauty; and, when the holydays are over, to be placed for frequent and affectionate consultation on a favourite shelf."—Athenæum.

Schiller's Lay of the Bell. Sir E. Bulwer Lytton's translation; beautifully illustrated by forty-two wood Engravings, drawn by Thomas Scott, and engraved by J. D. Cooper, after the Etchings by Retszch. Oblong 4to. cloth extra, 14*s*.; morocco, 25*s*.

An Entirely New Edition of Edgar A. Poe's Poems. Illustrated by Eminent Artists. Small 4to. cloth extra, price 10*s*. 6*d*.

A History of Lace, from the Earliest Period; with upwards of One Hundred Illustrations and Coloured Designs. By Mrs. Bury Palliser. One volume, 8vo. choicely bound in cloth. 31*s*. 6*d*.

The Royal Cookery Book. By Jules Gouffé, Chef de Cuisine of the Paris Jockey Club. Translated and Adapted for English use. By Alphonse Gouffé, Head Pastrycook to Her Majesty the Queen. Illustrated with large Plates beautifully printed in Colours, and One Hundred and Sixty-One Woodcuts. One volume, super-royal 8vo. cloth extra, 2*l*. 2*s*.

The Bayard Series.

CHOICE COMPANIONABLE BOOKS
FOR HOME AND ABROAD,

COMPRISING

HISTORY, BIOGRAPHY, TRAVEL, ESSAYS, NOVELETTES, ETC.

Which, under an Editor of known taste and ability, will be very choicely printed at the Chiswick Press; with Vignette Title-page, Notes, and Index; the aim being to insure permanent value, as well as present attractiveness, and to render each volume an acquisition to the libraries of a new generation of readers. Size, a handsome 16mo. bound flexible in cloth extra, gilt edges, averaging about 220 pages.

Each Volume, complete in itself, price Half-a-crown.

THE STORY OF THE CHEVALIER BAYARD. From the French of the Loyal Servant, M. de Berville, and others. By E. Walford. With Introduction and Notes by the Editor.

> " Praise of him must walk the earth
> For ever, and to noble deeds give birth.
> This is the happy warrior; this is he
> That every man in arms would wish to be."—*Wordsworth.*

SAINT LOUIS, KING OF FRANCE. The curious and characteristic Life of this Monarch by De Joinville. Translated by James Hutton.

> " *St. Louis and his companions, as described by Joinville, not only in their glistening armour, but in their every-day attire, are brought nearer to us, become intelligible to us, and teach us lessons of humanity which we can learn from men only, and not from saints and heroes. Here lies the real value of real history. It widens our minds and our hearts, and gives us that true knowledge of the world and of human nature in all its phases which but few can gain in the short span of their own life, and in the narrow sphere of their friends and enemies. We can hardly imagine a better book for boys to read or for men to ponder over.*"—Times.

The Bayard Series,—

THE ESSAYS OF ABRAHAM COWLEY. Comprising all his Prose Works; the Celebrated Character of Cromwell, Cutter of Coleman Street, &c. &c. With Life, Notes, and Illustrations by Dr. Hurd and others. Newly edited.

"*Praised in his day as a great Poet; the head of the school of poets called metaphysical, he is now chiefly known by those prose essays, all too short, and all too few, which, whether for thought or for expression, have rarely been excelled by any writer in any language.*"—Mary Russell Mitford's Recollections.

"*Cowley's prose stamps him as a man of genius, and an improver of the English language.*"—Thos. Campbell.

ABDALLAH AND THE FOUR-LEAVED SHAMROCK. By Edouard Laboullaye, of the French Academy. Translated by Mary L. Booth.

One of the noblest and purest French stories ever written.

TABLE-TALK AND OPINIONS OF NAPOLEON THE FIRST.

A compilation from the best sources of this great man's shrewd and often prophetic thoughts, forming the best inner life of the most extraordinary man of modern times.

VATHEK, by William Beckford.

In preparation.

CAVALIER AND PURITAN SONGS, by Henry Morley.

"*If the publishers go on as they have begun, they will have furnished us with one of the most valuable and attractive series of books that have ever been issued from the press.*"—Sunday Times.

"*There has, perhaps, never been produced anything more admirable either as regards matter or manner.*"—Oxford Times.

"'*The Bayard Series' is a perfect marvel of cheapness and of exquisite taste in the binding and getting up. We hope and believe that these delicate morsels of choice literature will be widely and gratefully welcomed.*"
              Nonconformist.

The Gentle Life Series.

Printed in Elzevir, on Toned Paper, and handsomely bound, forming suitable Volumes for Presents.

Price 6s. each; or in calf extra, price 10s. 6d.

I.

THE GENTLE LIFE. Essays in Aid of the Formation of Character of Gentlemen and Gentlewomen. Seventh Edition.

"*His notion of a gentleman is of the noblest and truest order. . . . . The volume is a capital specimen of what may be done by honest reason, high feeling, and cultivated intellect. . . . A little compendium of cheerful philosophy.*"—Daily News.

"*Deserves to be printed in letters of gold, and circulated in every house.*"—Chambers's Journal.

"*The writer's object is to teach people to be truthful, sincere, generous: to be humble-minded, but bold in thought and action.*"—Spectator.

"*Full of truth and persuasiveness, the book is a valuable composition, and one to which the reader will often turn for companionship.*"—Morning Post.

"*It is with the more satisfaction that we meet with a new essayist who delights without the smallest pedantry to quote the choicest wisdom of our forefathers, and who abides by those old-fashioned Christian ideas of duty which Steele and Addison, wits and men of the world, were not ashamed to set before the young Englishmen of 1713.*"—London Review.

II.

ABOUT IN THE WORLD. Essays by the Author of "The Gentle Life."

"*It is not easy to open it at any page without finding some happy idea.*" Morning Post.

"*Another characteristic merit of these essays is, that they make it their business, gently but firmly, to apply the qualifications and the corrections, which all philanthropic theories, all general rules or maxims, or principles, stand in need of before you can make them work.*"—Literary Churchman.

III.

FAMILIAR WORDS. An Index Verborum, or Quotation Handbook. Affording an immediate Reference to Phrases and Sentences that have become embedded in the English langnage. Second and enlarged Edition.

"*Should be on every library table, by the side of 'Roget's Thesaurus.'*" —Daily News.

"*Almost every familiar quotation is to be found in this work, which forms a book of reference absolutely indispensable to the literary man, and of interest and service to the public generally. Mr. Friswell has our best thanks for his painstaking, laborious, and conscientious work.*"—City Press.

IV.

LIKE UNTO CHRIST. A new translation of the "De Imitatione Christi," usually ascribed to Thomas à Kempis. With a Vignette from an Original Drawing by Sir Thomas Lawrence.

"*Think of the little work of Thomas à Kempis, translated into a hundred languages, and sold by millions of copies, and which, in inmost moments of deep thought, men make the guide of their hearts, and the friend of their closets.*"—Archbishop of York, at the Literary Fund, 1865.

V.

ESSAYS BY MONTAIGNE. Edited, Compared, Revised, and Annotated by the Author of "The Gentle Life." With Vignette Portrait.

"*The reader really gets in a compact form all of the charming, chatty Montaigne that he needs to know.*"—Observer.

"*We should be glad if any words of ours could help to bespeak a large circulation for this handsome attractive book; and who can refuse his homage to the good-humoured industry of the editor.*"—Illustrated Times.

VI.

THE COUNTESS OF PEMBROKE'S ARCADIA. Written by Sir Philip Sidney. Edited, with Notes, by the Author of "The Gentle Life." Dedicated, by permission, to the Earl of Derby. 7s. 6d.

"*All the best things in the Arcadia are retained intact in Mr. Friswell's edition, and even brought into greater prominence than in the original, by the curtailment of some of its inferior portions, and the omission of most of its eclogues and other metrical digressions*"—Examiner.

"*The book is now presented to the modern reader in a shape the most likely to be acceptable in these days of much literature and fastidious taste.*"—Daily News.

"*It was in itself a thing so interesting as a development of English literature, that we are thankful to Mr. Friswell for reproducing, in a very elegant volume, the chief work of the gallant and chivalrous, the gay yet learned knight, who patronized the muse of Spenser, and fell upon the bloody field of Zutphen, leaving behind him a light of heroism and humane compassion which would shed an eternal glory on his name, though all he ever wrote had perished with himself.*"—London Review.

VII.

THE GENTLE LIFE. Second Series.

"*There is the same mingled power and simplicity which makes the author so emphatically a first-rate essayist, giving a fascination in each essay which will make this volume at least as popular as its elder brother.*" Star.

"*These essays are amongst the best in our language.*"—Public Opinion.

VIII.

VARIA: Readings from Rare Books. Reprinted, by permission, from the *Saturday Review, Spectator*, &c.

CONTENTS:—The Angelic Doctor, Nostradamus, Thomas à Kempis, Dr. John Faustus, Quevedo, Mad. Guyon, Paracelsus, Howell the Traveller, Michael Scott, Lodowick Muggleton, Sir Thomas Browne, George Psalmanazar, The Highwaymen, The Spirit World.

"*The books discussed in this volume are no less valuable than they are rare, but life is not long enough to allow a reader to wade through such thick folios, and therefore the compiler is entitled to the gratitude of the public for having sifted their contents, and thereby rendered their treasures available to the general reader.*"—Observer.

IX.

A CONCORDANCE OR VERBAL INDEX to the whole of Milton's Poetical Works. Comprising upwards of 20,000 References. By Charles D. Cleveland, LL.D. With Vignette Portrait of Milton.

*** This work affords an immediate reference to any passage in any edition of Milton's Poems, to which it may be justly termed an indispensable Appendix.

"*An invaluable Index, which the publishers have done a public service in reprinting.*"—Notes and Queries.

X.

THE SILENT HOUR: Essays, Original and Selected. By the Author of "The Gentle Life."

CONTENTS.

How to read the Scriptures	From the Homilies.
Unreasonable Infidelity	Isaac Barrow.
The Great Loss of the Worldling	Richard Baxter.
Certainty of Death	Dean Sherlock.
On the Greatness of God	Massillon.
Our Daily Bread	Bishop Latimer.
The Art of Contentment	Archbishop Sandys.
The Foolish Exchange	Jeremy Taylor.
Of a Peaceable Temper	Isaac Barrow.
On the Marriage Ring	Jeremy Taylor.
Nearer to God	Archbishop Sandys.
The Sanctity of Home	John Ruskin.
The Thankful Heart	Isaak Walton.
Silence, Meditation, and Rest.	

And other Essays by the Editor. Second Edition. Nearly ready.

LITERATURE, WORKS OF REFERENCE ETC.

The Origin and History of the English Language, and of the early literature it embodies. By the Hon. George P. Marsh, U. S. Minister at Turin, Author of "Lectures on the English Language." 8vo. cloth extra, 16s.

Lectures on the English Language; forming the Introductory Series to the foregoing Work. By the same Author. 8vo. Cloth, 16s. This is the only author's edition.

Man and Nature; or, Physical Geography as Modified by Human Action. By George P. Marsh, Author of "Lectures on the English Language," &c. 8vo. cloth, 14s.

"*Mr. Marsh, well known as the author of two of the most scholarly works yet published on the English language, sets himself in excellent spirit, and with immense learning, to indicate the character, and, approximately, the extent of the changes produced by human action in the physical condition of the globe we inhabit. In four divisions of his work, Mr. Marsh traces the history of human industry as shown in the extensive modification and extirpation of animal and vegetable life in the woods, the waters, and the sands; and, in a concluding chapter, he discusses the probable and possible geographical changes yet to be wrought. The whole of Mr. Marsh's book is an eloquent showing of the duty of care in the establishment of harmony between man's life and the forces of nature, so as to bring to their highest points the fertility of the soil, the vigour of the animal life, and the salubrity of the climate, on which we have to depend for the physical well-being of mankind.*"—Examiner.

Her Majesty's Mails: a History of the Post Office, and an Industrial Account of its Present Condition. By Wm. Lewins, of the General Post Office. 2nd edition, revised, and enlarged, with a Photographic Portrait of Sir Rowland Hill. Small post 8vo. 6s.

"*Will take its stand as a really useful book of reference on the history of the Post. We heartily recommend it as a thoroughly careful performance.*"—Saturday Review.

A History of Banks for Savings; including a full account of the origin and progress of Mr. Gladstone's recent prudential measures. By William Lewins, Author of "Her Majesty's Mails." 8vo. cloth. 12s.

The English Catalogue of Books: giving the date of publication of every book published from 1835 to 1863, in addition to the title, size, price, and publisher, in one alphabet. An entirely new work, combining the Copyrights of the "London Catalogue" and the "British Catalogue." One thick volume of 900 pages, half morocco, 45s.

Index to the Subjects of Books published in the United Kingdom during the last Twenty Years—1837-1857. Containing as many as 74,000 references, under subjects, so as to ensure immediate reference to the books on the subject required, each giving title, price, publisher, and date. Two valuable Appendices are also given—A, containing full lists of all Libraries, Collections, Series, and Miscellanies—and B, a List of Literary Societies, Printing Societies, and their Issues. One vol. royal 8vo. Morocco, 1*l.* 6*s.*

A Dictionary of Photography, on the Basis of Sutton's Dictionary. Rewritten by Professor Dawson, of King's College, Editor of the "Journal of Photography;" and Thomas Sutton, B.A., Editor of "Photograph Notes." 8vo. with numerous Illustrations. 8*s.* 6*d.*

Dr. Worcester's New and Greatly Enlarged Dictionary of the English Language. Adapted for Library or College Reference, comprising 40,000 Words more than Johnson's Dictionary, and 250 pages more than the Quarto Edition of Webster's Dictionary. In one Volume, royal 4to. cloth, 1,834 pp. price 31*s.* 6*d.* Half russia, 2*l.* 2*s.* The Cheapest Book ever published.

"The volumes before us show a vast amount of diligence; but with Webster it is diligence in combination with fancifulness,—with Worcester in combination with good sense and judgment. Worcester's is the soberer and safer book, and may be pronounced the best existing English Lexicon."—*Athenæum.*

The Publishers' Circular, and General Record of British and Foreign Literature; giving a transcript of the title-page of every work published in Great Britain, and every work of interest published abroad, with lists of all the publishing houses.

Published regularly on the 1st and 15th of every Month, and forwarded post free to all parts of the world on payment of 8*s.* per annum.

A Handbook to the Charities of London. By Sampson Low, Jun. Comprising an Account of upwards of 800 Institutions chiefly in London and its Vicinity. A Guide to the Benevolent and to the Unfortunate. Cloth limp, 1*s.* 6*d.*

Prince Albert's Golden Precepts. *Second Edition,* with Photograph. A Memorial of the Prince Consort; comprising Maxims and Extracts from Addresses of His late Royal Highness. Many now for the first time collected and carefully arranged. With an Index. Royal 16mo. beautifully printed on toned paper, cloth, gilt edges, 2*s.* 6*d.*

Our Little Ones in Heaven: Thoughts in Prose and Verse, selected from the Writings of favourite Authors; with Frontispiece after Sir Joshua Reynolds. Fcap. 8vo. cloth extra, 3*s.* 6*d.*

Rural Essays. With Practical Hints on Farming and Agricul- tural Architecture. By Ik. Marvel, Author of "Reveries of a Bachelor." 1 vol. post 8vo. with numerous Illustrations. 8*s.*

The Book of the Hand; or, the Science of Modern Palmistry. Chiefly according to the Systems of D'Arpentigny and Desbarolles. By A. R. Craig, M.A. Crown 8vo. 7*s.* 6*d.*

BIOGRAPHY, TRAVEL, AND ADVENTURE.

THE Life of John James Audubon, the Naturalist, including his Romantic Adventures in the back woods of America, Correspondence with celebrated Europeans, &c. Edited, from materials supplied by his widow, by Robert Buchanan. 8vo. [*Shortly.*

Christian Heroes in the Army and Navy. By Charles Rogers, LL.D. Author of "Lyra Britannica." Crown 8vo. 3s. 6d.

Leopold the First, King of the Belgians; from unpublished documents, by Theodore Juste. Translated by Robert Black, M.A. [*In preparation.*

Fredrika Bremer's Life, Letters, and Posthumous Works. Edited by her sister, Charlotte Bremer; translated from the Swedish by Fred. Milow. Post 8vo. cloth. 10s. 6d.

The Rise and Fall of the Emperor Maximilian: an Authentic History of the Mexican Empire, 1861-7. Together with the Imperial Correspondence. With Portrait, 8vo. price 10s. 6d.

Madame Recamier, Memoirs and Correspondence of. Translated from the French and edited by J. M. Luyster. With Portrait. Crown 8vo. 7s. 6d.

Plutarch's Lives. An entirely new Library Edition, carefully revised and corrected, with some Original Translations by the Editor. Edited by A. H. Clough, Esq. sometime Fellow of Oriel College, Oxford, and late Professor of English Language and Literature at University College. 5 vols. 8vo. cloth. 2l. 10s.

Social Life of the Chinese: a Daguerreotype of Daily Life in China. Condensed from the Work of the Rev. J. Doolittle, by the Rev. Paxton Hood. With above 100 Illustrations. Post 8vo. price 8s. 6d.

The Open Polar Sea: a Narrative of a Voyage of Discovery towards the North Pole. By Dr. Isaac I. Hayes. An entirely new and cheaper edition. With Illustrations. Small post 8vo. 6s.

The Physical Geography of the Sea and its Meteorology; or, the Economy of the Sea and its Adaptations, its Salts, its Waters, its Climates, its Inhabitants, and whatever there may be of general interest in its Commercial Uses or Industrial Pursuits. By Commander M. F. Maury, LL.D. Tenth Edition. With Charts. Post 8vo. cloth extra, 5s.

Captain Hall's Life with the Esquimaux. New and cheaper Edition, with Coloured Engravings and upwards of 100 Woodcuts. With a Map. Price 7s. 6d. cloth extra. Forming the cheapest and most popular Edition of a work on Arctic Life and Exploration ever published.

"*This is a very remarkable book, and unless we very much misunderstand both him and his book, the author is one of those men of whom great nations do well to be proud.*"—Spectator.

The Black Country and its Green Border Land; or, Expeditions and Explorations round Birmingham, Wolverhampton, &c. By Elihu Burritt. 8vo. cloth, price 12s.

A Walk from London to John O'Groats, and from London to the Land's End and Back. With Notes by the Way. By Elihu Burritt. Two vols. price 6s. each, with Illustrations.

"*No one can take up this book without reading it through. We had thought that Elihu Burritt's 'Walk to John O'Groat's House' was the most perfect specimen of its kind that had ever seen the light, so genial, lively, and practical were the details he had brought together; but he has beaten his former literary production out of the field by this additional evidence of acuteness, impartiality, and good sound sense.*"—Bell's Weekly Messenger.

The Voyage Alone; a Sail in the "Yawl, Rob Roy." By John M'Gregor, Author of "A Thousand Miles in the Rob Roy Canoe." With Illustrations. Price 5s.

A Thousand Miles in the Rob Roy Canoe, on Rivers and Lakes of Europe. By John M'Gregor, M.A. Fifth edition. With a Map, and numerous Illustrations. Fcap. 8vo. cloth. Price 5s.

The Rob Roy on the Baltic. A Canoe Voyage in Norway, Sweden, &c. By John Macgregor, M.A. With a Map and numerous Illustrations. Fcap. 8vo. Price 5s.

NEW BOOKS FOR YOUNG PEOPLE.

STORIES of the Gorilla Country, narrated for Young People, by Paul Du Chaillu, author of "Discoveries in Equatorial Africa," &c. Small post 8vo. with 36 original Illustrations, 6s.

"*It would be hard to find a more interesting book for boys than this.*"—Times.

"*Young people will obtain from it a very considerable amount of information touching the manners and customs, ways and means of Africans, and of course great amusement in the accounts of the Gorilla. The book is really a meritorious work, and is elegantly got up.*"—Athenæum.

Life amongst the North and South American Indians. By George Catlin. And Last Rambles amongst the Indians beyond the Rocky Mountains and the Andes. With numerous Illustrations by the Author. 2 vols. small post 8vo. 5s. each, cloth extra.

"*An admirable book, full of useful information, wrapt up in stories peculiarly adapted to rouse the imagination and stimulate the curiosity of boys and girls. To compare a book with 'Robinson Crusoe,' and to say that it sustains such comparison, is to give it high praise indeed.*"—Athenæum.

List of Publications. 13

The Marvels of Optics. By F. Marion. Translated and edited by C. W. Quin. With 60 Illustrations. Cloth extra. 5s.

"*A most instructive and entertaining volume, comprising not only a carefully-written and popular account of the phenomena of vision and the laws of light, as illustrated by the latest discoveries and experiments of our wise men, but a history of 'Natural Magic' from its earliest to its latest wonders.*"—Observer.

Also uniform.

Thunder and Lightning. From the French of De Fonvielle, by D. T. L. Phipson. With 38 full-page Woodcuts. 5s.

Alwyn Morton; his School and his Schoolfellows. A Story of St. Nicholas' Grammar School. Illustrated. Fcap. 8vo. 5s.

The Silver Skates; a Story of Holland Life. Edited by W. H. G. Kingston. Illustrated, small post 8vo. cloth extra, 3s. 6d.

The Voyage of the Constance; a tale of the Polar Seas. By Mary Gillies. New Edition, with 8 Illustrations by Charles Keene. Fcap. 3s. 6d.

The Boy's Own Book of Boats. A Description of every Craft that sails upon the waters; and how to Make, Rig, and Sail Model Boats, by W. H. G. Kingston, with numerous Illustrations by E. Weedon. Second edition, enlarged. Fcap. 8vo. 3s. 6d.

"*This well-written, well-wrought book.*"—Athenæum.

Also by the same Author,

Ernest Bracebridge: or, Boy's Own Book of Sports. 3s. 6d.
The Fire Ships. A Story of the Days of Lord Cochrane. 5s.
The Cruise of the Frolic. 5s.
Jack Buntline: the Life of a Sailor Boy. 2s.

The True History of Dame Perkins and her Grey Mare, and their run with the Hounds. Told for the Countryside and the Fireside. By Linden Meadows. With Eight Coloured Illustrations by Phiz. Small 4to. cloth, 5s.

Great Fun Stories. Told by Thomas Hood and Thomas Archer to 48 coloured pictures of Edward Wehnert. Beautifully printed in colours, 10s. 6d. Plain, 6s. well bound in cloth, gilt edges.

Or in Eight separate books, 1s. each, coloured. 6d. plain.

The Cherry-coloured Cat. The Live Rocking-Horse. Master Mischief. Cousin Nellie. Harry High-Stepper. Grandmamma's Spectacles. How the House was Built. Dog Toby.

Great Fun and More Fun for our Little Friends. By Harriet Myrtle. With Edward Wehnert's Pictures. 2 vols. each 5s.

A Book of Laughter for Young and Old.

A Bushel of Merry-Thoughts, by Wilhelm Busch. Including the Naughty Boys of Corinth, the Children that took the Sugar Cake, Ice Peter, &c. Annotated and Ornamented by Harry Rogers, plain 2s 6d.; coloured 3s. 6d.

Under the Waves; or the Hermit Crab in Society. By Annie E. Ridley. Impl. 16mo. cloth extra, with coloured illustration Cloth, 4s.; gilt edges, 4s. 6d.

Also beautifully Illustrated:—

Little Bird Red and Little Bird Blue. Coloured, 5s.
Snow-Flakes, and what they told the Children. Coloured, 5s.
Child's Book of the Sagacity of Animals. 5s.; or coloured, 7s. 6d.
Child's Picture Fable Book. 5s.; or coloured, 7s. 6d.
Child's Treasury of Story Books. 5s.; or coloured, 7s. 6d.
The Nursery Playmate. 200 Pictures. 5s.; or coloured, 9s.

Golden Hour; a Story for Young People. By Sir Lascelles Wraxall, Bart. With Eight full page Illustrations, 5s.

Also, same price, full of Illustrations:—

Black Panther; a Boy's Adventures among the Red Skins.
Stanton Grange; or, Boy Life at a Private Tutor's. By the Rev. C. J. Atkinson.

Paul Duncan's Little by Little; a Tale for Boys. Edited by Frank Freeman. With an Illustration by Charles Keene. Fcap. 8vo. cloth 2s.; gilt edges, 2s. 6d. Also, same price,

Boy Missionary; a Tale for Young People. By Mrs. J. M. Parker.
Difficulties Overcome. By Miss Brightwell.
The Babes in the Basket: a Tale in the West Indian Insurrection.
Jack Buntline; the Life of a Sailor Boy. By W. H. G. Kingston.

The Swiss Family Robinson; or, the Adventures of a Father and Mother and Four Sons on a Desert Island. With Explanatory Notes and Illustrations. First and Second Series. New Edition, complete in one volume, 3s. 6d.

Geography for my Children. By Mrs. Harriet Beecher Stowe. Author of "Uncle Tom's Cabin," &c. Arranged and Edited by an English Lady, under the Direction of the Authoress. With upwards of Fifty Illustrations. Cloth extra, 4s. 6d.

Stories of the Woods; or, the Adventures of Leather-Stocking: A Book for Boys, compiled from Cooper's Series of "Leather-Stocking Tales." Fcap. cloth, Illustrated, 5s.

Child's Play. Illustrated with Sixteen Coloured Drawings by E. V. B., printed in fac-simile by W. Dickes' process, and ornamented with Initial Letters. New edition, with India paper tints, royal 8vo. cloth extra, bevelled cloth, 7s. 6d. The Original Edition of this work was published at One Guinea.

BELLES LETTRES, FICTION, &c.

DAVID GRAY; and other Essays, chiefly on Poetry. By Robert Buchanan, author of "London Poems," "North Coast," &c. In one vol. fcap. 8vo. price 6s.

"*The book is one to possess as well as read, not only for the biographical essay on David Gray,—an essay of much more than deep interest, of rare power, and a strange unimpassioned pathos,—but also for certain passages of fine original criticism, occurring in essays—thickly sprinkled, we admit, with foreign substances—on poetry, and the religion and aims which modern poets should put before them.*"—Spectator.

The Book of the Sonnet; being Selections, with an Essay on Sonnets and Sonneteers. By the late Leigh Hunt. Edited, from the original MS. with Additions, by S. Adams Lee. 2 vols. price 18s.

"*Reading a book of this sort should make us feel proud of our language and of our literature, and proud also of that cultivated common nature which can raise so many noble thoughts and images out of this hard, sullen world into a thousand enduring forms of beauty. The 'Book of the Sonnet' should be a classic, and the professor as well as the student of English will find it a work of deep interest and completeness.*"—London Review.

English and Scotch Ballads, &c. An extensive Collection. Designed as a Complement to the Works of the British Poets, and embracing nearly all the Ancient and Traditionary Ballads both of England and Scotland, in all the important varieties of form in which they are extant, with Notices of the kindred Ballads of other Nations. Edited by F. J. Child, new Edition, revised by the Editor. 8 vols. fcap. cloth, 3s. 6d. each.

The Autocrat of the Breakfast Table. By Oliver Wendell Holmes, LL.D. Popular Edition, 1s. Illustrated Edition, choicely printed, cloth extra, 6s.

The Professor at the Breakfast Table. By Oliver Wendell Holmes, Author of "The Autocrat of the Breakfast-Table." Cheap Edition fcap 3s. 6d.

"*A welcome book. It may be taken up again and again, and its pages paused over for the enjoyment of the pleasant touches and suggestive passages which they contain.*"—Athenæum.

The Guardian Angel: a Romance. By the Author of "The Autocrat of the Breakfast Table." Second Edition. 2 vols. post 8vo.

Bee-Keeping. By "The Times" Bee-master. Small post 8vo. numerous Illustrations, cloth, 5s.

"*Our friend the Bee-master has the knack of exposition, and knows how to tell a story well; over and above which, he tells a story so that thousands can take a practical, and not merely a speculative interest in it.*"—Times.

The Rooks' Garden, and other Papers. By Cuthbert Bede, Author of "The Adventures of Mr. Verdant Green." Cheap Edition. Post 8vo. cloth, gilt edges. 3s. 6d.

The White Wife; with other stories, Supernatural, Romantic and Legendary. Collected and Illustrated by Cuthbert Bede. Post 8vo. cloth, 6s. Cheap Edition, fancy boards, 2s. 6d.

Queer Little People. By the Author of "Uncle Tom's Cabin."
Fcap. 1s. *Also by the same Author.*

The Little Foxes that Spoil the Grapes, 1s.
House and Home Papers, 1s.
The Pearl of Orr's Island, Illustrated by Gilbert, 5s.
The Minister's Wooing. Illustrated by Phiz, 5s.

Entertaining and Excellent Stories for Young Ladies, 3s. 6d. each, cloth, gilt edges.

Helen Felton's Question: a Book for Girls. By Agnes Wylde.
Faith Gartney's Girlhood. By Mrs. D. T. Whitney. Seventh thousand.
The Gayworthys. By the same Author. Third Edition.
A Summer in Leslie Goldthwaite's Life. By the same Author.
The Masque at Ludlow. By the Author of "Mary Powell."
Miss Biddy Frobisher: a Salt Water Story. By the same Author.
Selvaggio; a Story of Italy. By the same Author. New Edition.
The Journal of a Waiting Gentlewoman. By a new Author. New Edition.
The Shady Side and the Sunny Side. Two Tales of New England. By Country Pastors' Wives.

"*Written with great power, and possesses a deep and captivating interest—an interest which will enchain the interest of all contemplative readers. We remember nothing in fictitious narrative so pathetic; we wish such books, and especially this book, to be read by everyone.*"
Standard.

Marian; or, the Light of Some One's Home. By Maud Jeanne Franc. Small post 8vo., 5s. *Also, by the same Author.*

Emily's Choice: an Australian Tale. 5s.
Vermont Vale: or, Home Pictures in Australia. 5s.

Each Volume, cloth flexible, 2s.; or sewed, 1s. 6d.

Tauchnitz's English Editions of German Authors. The following are now ready:—

1. On the Heights. By B. Auerbach. 3 vols.
2. In the Year '13. By Fritz Reuter. 1 vol.
3. Faust. By Goethe. 1 vol.
4. Undine, and other Tales. By Fouqué. 1 vol.
5. L'Arrabiata. By Paul Heyse. 1 vol.
6. The Princess, and other Tales. By Heinrich Zschokke. 1 vol.

Other volumes are in preparation.

LONDON: SAMPSON LOW, SON, AND MARSTON,

CROWN BUILDINGS, 188, FLEET STREET.

English, American, and Colonial Booksellers and Publishers.

Chiswick Press:—Whittingham and Wilkins, Tooks Court, Chancery Lane.

APR 2 1895

FEB 26 1896

MAR 2 1897

JAN 4 1904

DUE NOV 26 1917

JUL 17 1922

DUE DEC 29 1922

MAY -7 1931

MAY -7 1931

BOUND BY
BURN & Co
KIRBY ST
E.C.